SUPERPOWER DOMINANCE AND MILITARY AID

A Study of Military Aid to Pakistan

SUPERPOWER DOMINANCE AND MILITARY AID

A Study of Military Aid to Pakistan

Baldev Raj Nayar

MANOHAR
1991

ISBN 81-85425-53-1

First Published 1991

Published by

Ajay Kumar Jain
Manohar Publications
2/6 Ansari Road, Daryaganj
New Delhi - 110 002

Printed at

Rajkamal Electric Press
B 35/9 G.T. Karnal Road
Industrial Area
Delhi - 110 033

Preface

This book was originally presented as a paper entitled "American Containment Policy and Regional Powers: Motivations and Diplomacy in the U.S. Decision on Military Aid to Pakistan, 1954" at the International Seminar on Afro Asian Geopolitics, Panjab University, Chandigarh, April 4-11, 1990. But I have been persuaded to seek a wider audience for the paper because its central ideas are of paramount significance to the understanding of the international politics of various regional systems, especially now that the globe has once again, as it entered the 1990s, been transformed into a unipolar world under American hegemony. The subject of this book, though narrower in focus, should be seen as but one illustration of a larger pattern in the relations between a single superpower and various regional powers. Indeed, the postwar history of the world has been played out as a drama of contest between that superpower and the regional powers. The consistent and uniform thread throughout this drama is the policy of containment implemented against those regional powers, even if this term is not always actually used and the containment takes different forms from region to region.

It is fitting that this book should be brought out by Ramesh Jain of Manohar, since it was he who originally published my booklength study *American Geopolitics and India*. That book was the first to look at Indo-U.S. relations not in terms of personality or ideological conflicts, but as rooted in a strategic conflict between a superpower and a regional power, a conflict built into the very structure of world power. I have been struck by the fact that American scholars who have viscerally disagreed with my interpretation have invariably failed to countenance the evidence adduced in support of it, or to provide any evidence in support of their disagreement. The present book, based on American documentation that has become available since the publication of the previous work, should serve as a vindication of the earlier unorthodox and revisionist interpretation.

I would like to thank my esteemed colleagues at McGill, Paul Noble, Patrick James, and Samuel J. Noumoff, in the Department of Political Science, and Jagdish Handa, in the Department of Economics, for their critical but valuable comments. I am similarly obliged to Mr. Anupam Sharma for his very helpful suggestions. James Nielson helped to prepare the text for publication. Special thanks are due to Professor M. M. Puri for inviting me to the International Seminar in the first place, and to Panjab University for its hospitality.

Montreal, March 1, 1991

Baldev Raj Nayar
McGill University

Contents

Introduction

The American decision in February 1954 to provide military aid to Pakistan for the modernisation and expansion of its armed forces, while perhaps of peripheral strategic importance from the perspective of the global concerns of American decision-makers, was a momentous development for the international politics of the Indian subcontinent. It constituted the first open intervention in the postwar period by a superpower in the affairs of the subcontinent, which had hitherto lain outside the central conflict between the blocs led by the two superpowers. The American decision soon generated a rivalry with the other superpower in the interstate politics of the region. In the process, the region was to a considerable degree integrated into the dynamics of the bipolar international system.

What were the motivations of the United States in undertaking this enormously important step in the South Asian region? The question merits re-examination in the light of the more recent publication of selected official documents for the period in the *Foreign Relations of the United States* (hereafter FR), some memoirs and secondary analyses. The conclusions of scholarship are not necessarily permanent, and need to be re-evaluated as new evidence becomes available. Accordingly, this study looks at the question of American motivations by examining (1) two salient but differing perspectives on the issue of American motivations; (2) the bearing of official and non-official evidence -- relating to the period around the time of the decision by the Eisenhower administration to extend military aid -- on the contention between the two perspectives; (3) the relevance of the intellectual baggage inherited by the Eisenhower administration; and (4) the diplomacy involved in the extension of military aid to Pakistan. An appendix discusses the nature of the new evidence and its use in the study.

Chapter One
The Contending Perspectives on Motivation

There seem to be two different perspectives on American motivations in the decision to provide military aid to Pakistan. The first of these basically represents the official public position of the United States government at the time of the American decision. It fundamentally argues that the decision had as its objective the assuring of collective defence for the region along with other regions against potential Soviet aggression.[1] The particular decision on Pakistan was then part and parcel of the general policy of the United States on the global *containment* of the Soviet Union. Under this perspective, the decision was not aimed against Pakistan's rival in the region -- India -- even though it may have had adverse consequences for the latter; America's good faith was amply displayed in the parallel simultaneous offer of military aid to India even as the US continued to provide economic aid to it.

A slight variant on this perspective continues to take the American decision to be an integral part of the containment policy aimed against the Soviet Union, but only with the narrower objective of obtaining military bases in Pakistan for

[1] See William J. Barnds, *India, Pakistan and the Major Powers* (New York: Praeger Publishers, 1972), pp. 83-97; Richard Sisson, "Pakistan and U.S. Foreign Policy Formulation: Interest, Perception, and the Context of Choice," in Leo E. Rose and Noor A. Husain (ed.), *United States-Pakistan Relations* (Berkeley, CA: Institute of East Asian Studies, University of California, 1985), pp. 110-27; and U.S. Department of State, *Bulletin*, XXX, no. 768 (March 15, 1954), pp. 400-401. See also John Lewis Gaddis, *Strategies of Containment: A Critical Appraisal of Postwar American National Security Policy* (New York: Oxford University Press, 1982), pp. 152-53

the purpose. The American military aid to Pakistan served merely as a necessary *quid pro quo* for American military bases.[2] Even then the United States undertook supposedly only a moderate and limited military aid programme, remained solicitous of India's interests through economic aid, and adopted by and large an evenhanded approach in the mutual disputes of the two regional rivals.

If the first perspective represents the conventional view, then the second but more revisionist perspective takes the American decision as being aimed not only against the Soviet bloc but also against India as the preeminent power in the region, which was intent on building an independent centre of power in the area, outside the sphere of influence of the United States. In other words, the target of the military aid was India, no less than it was the Soviet Union.[3]

Although differentiated, the two perspectives obviously share some common ground. The second perspective does not necessarily dispute the notion, which is the centrepiece of the first perspective, that military aid to Pakistan may have been directed against the Soviet Union. It would be extraordinarily foolhardy to deny the impact on US policy for the region of what had become the single most important geopolitical concern in the American posture toward the world -- the containment of the Soviet Union as the occupant of the Mackinderian heartland through a Spykmanian military organisation under American leadership of the rimlands, of which South Asia is a part. It would thus seem consistent with its policy of containment for the United States -- especially as it moved from "strongpoint defence" to "perimeter defence" after NSC-68, more particularly in the

[2] M.S. Venkataramani, *The American Role in Pakistan* (New Delhi: Radiant Publishers, 1983). For sheer industry in archival research, this study has few rivals in scholarship on Pakistan.

[3] Baldev Raj Nayar, "A World Role: The Dialectics of Purpose and Power," in John W. Mellor (ed.), *India: A Rising Middle Power* (Boulder, Colorado: Westview Press, 1979), ch. 5.

wake of the Korean war[4] – to build up militarily those areas, such as Pakistan, which were ready and willing to join in the collective enterprise of containing the Soviet bloc. The question that arises distinctively with the second perspective, however, is whether there were other additional motives relating specifically to the subcontinent's principal power, India – that is, containment of India.

Notwithstanding their shared elements, the two perspectives differ profoundly in their assumptions about the state behaviour of the United States in the postwar international system. The first perspective takes the American policy of containment to be reactive, inspired primarily by the changed structure of the international environment in the aftermath of World War II. In that view, the postwar world saw the rise of a tremendously powerful but territorially expansionist power in the shape of the Soviet Union, fired at the same time by the fervent messianic ideology of communism to pursue an imperialist course. On the other hand, traditionally isolationist, disdainfully opposed to the power politics of Europe, and fearful of entangling alliances, the United States was perforce, in the absence of any other viable great power, compelled to assume the burden of world leadership. It was compelled to do so for no other reason except the idealistic one to preserve the peace against the aggressive designs and pressures of international communism on the weaker states around the periphery of the Soviet bloc. Designed to protect the diversity of the world, American intentions in assuming leadership were benign, just as they had been in the American intervention in the two great wars of the 20th century to save the world from autocracy and totalitarianism.

In contrast, the second perspective has little place for claims to exceptionalism in terms of noble motives on the part of states, while it sees their international behaviour governed

[4] See Gaddis, pp. 57-58, 89-126.

by a universally operative "security dilemma".[5] Not taking the US to be immune to the processes that accompany the ensuing struggle for power among nations, it applies to the understanding of American behaviour the very same paradigm of realism that has been dominant in mainstream American scholarship in the study of the state behaviour of other nations, including the Soviet Union. In the conflictual international system that results from the security dilemma, the behaviour of states is seen as a function of their power. Given the large number of states in the international hierarchy, their behaviour can be more easily comprehended by distinguishing three major types among them, each with characteristically different modes of state behaviour corresponding to their power position: great powers, middle powers, and minor powers. This distinction is basic to the alternative interpretation of the American decision to arm Pakistan, and therefore requires elaboration as an analytical framework.

Analytical Framework on Great Power-Middle Power Interaction

Great powers command a "subject" role in the international system where, as part of the dominant power structure, they make in competition or collusion the vital decisions about the fate and destiny of that system. In the present epoch, the full-fledged status of great powers has been the prerogative of the United States and the Soviet Union; China as a nuclear power of subcontinental size is considered a candidate great power.

[5] As is obvious, this study falls in the tradition of realism, which I take to be the regnant paradigm in North America, if not the world. Even those who are of the behavioural persuasion carry, in actual fact, realist assumptions in their understanding of the functioning of the international system. There are likely, however, to be harder and softer versions of realism.

In contrast, minor powers with "object" status have limited foreign policy autonomy, they are at the receiving end of the decisions made by the great powers, and their lot is often to adapt as best as possible to the decisions of the subject powers. On the other hand, with an in-between status, middle powers as actual or aspirant independent centres of power, while without sufficient leverage to influence the course of the international system, do possess enough capabilities to have, within a given configuration of power, a considerable degree of foreign policy autonomy and the capacity to resist the application of unwelcome decisions, especially in the realm of security. Whereas great powers have system-wide or global influence, independent centres of power are often dominant or preeminent in a certain region; thus they are often also referred to as regional powers. Middle powers often tend to erect on the foundation of their regional dominance or preeminence a claim to some role at the global level.

Contrary impulses motivate the great powers and middle powers in their state behaviour. Typically, a great power resists the emergence of new great powers, for to accommodate others to a similar role is to diminish one's own power, and to that extent lose some control over one's own national security and welfare. Rather, the tendency for the great power is to extend its power as far as possible, to exercise dominion over others, and to reduce middle powers to the status of objects. A particularly interesting contemporary manifestation of this tendency has been the attempt by a concert of the great powers to block nuclear proliferation, which would have added to the power of the middle powers and thus reduced that of the great powers.

On the other hand, for those middle powers that have the potential, entrance into the exclusive club of subjects is also a compelling goal. This is so not simply for status or prestige purposes, but for national survival and welfare, for middle powers are constantly confronted with the prospect of domination by the great powers. The consequence of the contrary impulses of great powers and middle powers is therefore often to set them on a collision course, and the graduation of a middle power to the status of great power is no journey along a smooth path but one whose story is usually written in blood and fire. Basically, however, middle powers act reactively and defensively; it is the great powers that have a prior and initiating role, and it is their policies therefore that compel attention.

Great powers, according to George Liska, typically choose from among three policies toward middle powers: containment, satellisation, and accommodation. On containment of middle powers, he notes: "Great powers can treat and have reason to treat individual middle powers as regional rivals, and be led to help still lesser states to contain them under the pretence of restraining, unilaterally or cooperatively, all Third World conflict."[6] The intent, of course, is to reduce the international influence of the middle power as a claimant to subject role, to subordinate its foreign policy to the requirements of the great power or to raise the costs of its foreign policy autonomy, and to prevent its rise to the status of a subject power. Not suprisingly, containment may lead to expansionism; indeed, expansionism is the other side of containment. The key mechanism in the containment of middle powers is the creation of a balance of power in the region favourable to the great power. Such a regional balance may be implemented through a policy of alliances, either tacit or explicit, or both, whereby the great power in one way or another aligns its influence and power with that of some local or extra-regional power to balance off the targeted middle power. This may also be supplemented by the direct military presence of the great power in the form of bases in the region. The policy of containment does not exclude bargaining; quite

[6] See George Liska, "The Third World: Regional Systems and Global Order," in Robert E. Osgood et al., *Retreat From Empire* (Baltimore: Johns Hopkins University Press, 1973), p. 226.

the contrary, its purpose is to achieve a position of "bargaining from strength" or to secure leverage.

Under a policy of satellisation, great powers regard middle powers "as regional allies in contest with other great powers and proceed to reinforce them competitively, possibly as a means to reapportionment by way of reclientisation."[7] The central mechanism in this policy is the acquisition of an interventionist capability in the internal and external affairs of a target country in order to provide the great power with leverage over the country's foreign policy. Satellisation operates through the creation of dependencies in other countries on the subject power. Its chief instruments are economic aid and military alliances, which are important for the penetration and dependence they make possible in crucial sectors of the targeted nation. Finally, in contrast there is the policy of accommodation under which great powers "proceed either unilaterally or jointly progressively to devolve regional responsibilities to apparently constructively disposed middle powers." A critical consideration for the superpowers here is whether the middle power is "loyalist" or "rebellious".[8] Iran in the 1970s was an example of power devolution as a surrogate for the US in the region.

There is no reason to attribute rigidity to this analytical framework describing the policies of containment, satellisation and accommodation. In the first place, these policies should be treated not as mutually exclusive categories but rather as central tendencies in the foreign policy posture of a great power, which may incorporate one or more such tendencies at any given time. Furthermore, implementation of any one of these policies can never be absolute, but requires sophistication and subtlety; containment of a middle power in one region, for example, may necessitate modifying or supplementing containment of another middle power

[7] *Ibid.*

[8] *Ibid.*

elsewhere. Nor do such policies remain static or permanent; changes in the distribution of power and the pattern of alliances and adversary relationships in the international system result in changes in superpower policies toward middle powers.

US Policy on Containment: Global and Regional

Considered in the light of this analytical framework, containment is of more general significance than, as often understood, the one specific historical application of the policy to the Soviet Union in contemporary times. However, that specific containment of the Soviet Union was to bring, in its train, serious implications for other powers, middle and minor. In the wake of World War II, the United States emerged not merely as one of two superpowers but the dominant superpower around which there developed an essentially unipolar system, notwithstanding claims about a bipolar system.[9] The development of such an international system followed necessarily from the American monopoly of the awesome power of the atom, its unrivalled economic power – matching that of the rest of the planet put together – its far-flung military power, with bases encircling the Soviet bloc, and its unchallenged control of the high seas. On the other hand, the Soviet Union – despite its rise to the status of a superpower and its territorial gains on its immediate borders – was an economically and demographically devastated power, and therefore militarily vulnerable and insecure.[10] With its

[9] This characterisation of the international system as unipolar pertains specifically to the first decade after the end of World War II, and not necessarily to the subsequent period. Although the characterisation may be debatable, it draws attention to the manifest preponderance and reach of US power at the *global* level.

[10] Gaddis highlights the point by stating that 53 Russians and 15 Germans died in the war for every one American who died. In an

new adversary, uniquely possessed of the atomic bomb and seeking to contest, if not altogether deny -- through its Open Door claims -- the fruits of victory against Germany, the Soviet Union cautiously tested the limits of its security arrangements on its borders and retreated when challenged. However, rather than treat its erstwhile ally as an equal, entitled to the same privileges as reserved for itself in regard to bases and access across international waterways, the United States -- consistent with its status as the dominant superpower -- applied the policy of containment to what was essentially a middle power, confined to its own immediate region, even as the US at times attempted its satellisation through the lure of economic aid.

Understood thus, containment of the Soviet Union was not simply a reactive phenomenon, but an activist policy, stemming out of the power position of the United States, of which the American leadership was not particularly unaware. The added ideology of anti-communism employed by the US in its endeavour at containment can be seen as merely serving an instrumental purpose for the mobilisation of domestic and international support, but was not integral to the policy. The ideological cast given to the Soviet challenge, in the context of power vacuums on the Soviet periphery in the wake of the decline of British imperial power, was not essential to the

interesting comment he raises the question if that might not have been the consequence of American design. Noting that Truman had in 1941 recommended that the US allow the Russians and Germans to kill each other off, and that Roosevelt kept postponing a western front despite Russian insistence, he asks, "whether something like this might not have been Roosevelt's intent all along: might his strategy in reality have been a crafty way of ensuring both full Russian participation in the war and the postwar containment of the Soviet Union, not by denying that country territory or resources, but by forcing it to exhaust itself." Although strenuously disputing such an interpretation, he adds: "With the elusive Roosevelt, one can never be sure.... if this had been his strategy, it is unlikely that he would have told anyone about it." Gaddis, p. 8.

policy of containment. Rather, the policy of containment was built into the accession of the US to the status of the dominant superpower; having achieved that status, it was but inevitable for the United States to take on the functions that went with it. Despite American opposition as a matter of principle to spheres of influence for others, most particularly the Soviet Union, the United States was propelled -- even if its decision-makers may have only dimly perceived it that way -- to attempt to convert the entire globe into its own sphere of influence. What had hitherto been only a regional sphere of influence on a smaller scale in Latin America -- long before the rise of communism -- was attempted to be transformed onto a global scale after the postwar rise of the US as a global power. As Morgenthau had maintained, the Monroe Doctrine was the "most comprehensive unilateral proclamation of a sphere of influence in modern times."[11] No special selfish or malign intent need be attributed to the US for such behaviour; it ought to be seen simply as a function of the accession of the US to the new power position of the dominant superpower.

As the overall approach suggests, the notion of containment need not necessarily be restricted to the Soviet Union, but is to be seen as available to a global power as a potential policy for application to all middle powers that refuse to submit to satellisation and aspire instead to the status of more or less independent centres of power. Indeed, it is a seriously mistaken view to restrict the notion of containment to what is but only one specific application: the containment of communism. Rather, the American policy of containment has had as its targets all independent centres of power. Liska argues in justification:

[11] Deborah Welch Larson, *Origins of Containment: A Psychological Explanation* (Princeton: Princeton University Press, 1985), p. 38. See also Lars Schoultz, *National Security and United States Policy toward Latin America* (Princeton: Princeton University Press, 1987), pp. 106-22.

> As long as the United States could be basically inspired by the norms proper to a globally pre-eminent world power, single-handedly upholding order in the several regions, the American attitude to potential regional imperialists had to be dogmatically negative. Middle-power self-assertion beyond a definite readily discernible point threatened to inhibit or bar US access to still lesser states in a region, while creating a problem for the credibility and appeal of American opposition to Communist-tinged expansionism.[12]

This claim to unrestricted access globally by the US, also referred to as "Open Door",[13] has usually translated itself into a claim for American domination in any given region, with the US emerging as the security manager of the region and the sole determinant of developments in the region. Even though the United States may often proclaim that it is merely trying to prevent the Soviet Union or some other power from becoming the dominant power in the region, the purpose is precisely for the US itself to become the dominant power of the region.

Behind this universal Open Door policy in the postwar period has been a messianic complex born of the emergence of the United States as the preeminent, indeed the only, global power at the end of World War II, ushering in what many believed to be the American Century or Pax Americana. Drew Middleton pointed out how after World War II, the United States envisioned "an unprecedented expansion of power and influence on a global scale," one "greater in extent than any known to history," and he underlined "the supreme

[12] George Liska, *States in Evolution: Changing Societies and Traditional Systems in World Politics* (Baltimore: Johns Hopkins University Press, 1973), p. 152.

[13] Robert W. Tucker, *The Radical Left and American Foreign Policy* (Baltimore: Johns Hopkins University Press, 1971), p. 66.

national confidence it promoted in the American people." He continued: "Americans were emboldened to believe that there were no policies they could not implement, no danger they could not overcome." Not until the military failure in Vietnam was there disillusionment with such power among "those internationalists who believed in an America destined to dominate Asia and the Pacific."[14] But until then, the sense of American omnipotence possessed most Americans. Dean Rusk gave expression to this feeling of power, saying, "When the United States applies pressure on something, anything, it gives."[15] As the hegemonic superpower, the United States aimed, then, to extend its influence, power and domination across the entire globe, restricting the Soviet Union to its own region for a considerable period of time. One State Department policy planning chief acknowledged: "In the period following World War II, our preeminent power encouraged us to believe we could shape the globe according to American designs."[16]

More generally, in relation to middle powers the United States has pursued the twin policies of satellisation and containment over most of the postwar period. There is an intimate relationship between these two policies. Where satellisation was resisted, containment has been pursued and, in the name of containment of some middle powers, the US has pursued the satellisation of others. In turn, successful containment persuaded some middle powers to cooperate with the United States; in other words, to become satellised.

The central mechanism in the containment of middle powers has been the creation in any given region of a balance of power favourable to the United States. The concept of

[14] Drew Middleton, *Retreat From Victory* (New York: Hawthorn Books, 1973), pp. 45-46, 213.

[15] Marvin Kalb and Bernard Kalb, *Kissinger* (Boston: Little, Brown and Co., 1974), p. 65.

[16] Winston Lord, "America's Purposes in an Ambiguous Age," *Department of State Bulletin*, No. 1845 (November 4, 1974), p. 617.

regional balances has been central to American foreign policy and, as James Chace pointed out, it often demands American intervention "to prevent the balance from being upset."[17] In 1974 Defence Secretary James Schlesinger gave a revealing expression both of the rationale for middle power containment and of its instruments. In testimony before the Senate Foreign Relations Committee, he stated that the military assistance programme in the form of sales, credits, and grants was "a part of the overall security programme of the United States," and went on to argue that "there are parts of the world in which the United States does not and will not have the manpower to intervene and, *in order to maintain a military balance in those parts of the world*, foreign military assistance plays a role which should be related to overall political and military strategy of the United States." He further noted that "in this way, we seek to *achieve regional stability* in crucial areas of the world without the need for direct intervention by American Forces."[18]

Listening to Schlesinger's statement, Senator Percy quickly grasped the underlying principle about "the necessity to establish *military balance* in critical areas of the world for the purpose of a general equilibrium in military power." He further raised a profound question: "Both you and Admiral Moorer speak of developing *regional balances*. Is it the basis of this theory to support one power in each region or to try to *maintain a parity in arms in each region*?" Schlesinger did not challenge the thrust of the question, nor did he dispute the notion of parity or building one power as a counterweight against another, but he rather stressed the subtlety with which policy had to be handled in this regard. Again, in 1975, in response to one subcommittee chairman's query about "the

[17] *New York Times*, September 13, 1976.

[18] U.S. Congress, Senate, Committee on Foreign Relations, *Foreign Assistance Authorisation*, Hearings, 93rd Congress, 2nd Session, 1974, pp. 192, 194, 195, 198. Emphasis added.

general guiding principles that govern our conduct in the sale of arms," a senior Defence Department official replied: "Balance is one of them."[19]

The logic of theory and the larger basis of American state behaviour alone ought to lead to the hypothesis of an American posture of containment toward regional powers, especially at a time when the US was the dominant, if not the singular, global power in the international system. The critical question remains, however, if there is evidence in support of this hypothesis.

[19] Amos Jordan, in U.S. Congress, House, Committee on International Relations, *The Persian Gulf, 1975*, Hearings, 94th Congress, 1st Session, 1975, pp. 88, 92, 93.

Chapter Two
Motives in the Eisenhower Administration

At first blush, it seems rather fanciful to contemplate India as a target for the application of containment. For, here was a nation just emergent from two centuries of colonial rule, a backward agricultural economy with mass poverty and subsistence standards of living, a weak and fragile state that appeared before the US as a supplicant for food and economic aid, and a peripheral country lying geographically beyond Iran and therefore of little strategic interest to the United States. Why would the United States be bothered at all about it, with its hands full with more important issues, such as massive retaliation, rolling back communism, liberation of captive peoples, agonising reappraisals, and brinkmanship! No wonder that any discussion of the idea of application of the concept of containment in relation to India brings on not only disdainful yawns and peremptory dismissal, but also the charge of its performing a psychological function for "natives" about the exaggerated importance of their country in international affairs.[1]

[1] See, for example, William J. Barnds and W. Howard Wriggins, in *Foreign Policy*, No. 20 (Fall 1975), pp. 250-53; Stephen P. Cohen and Richard L. Park, *India: Emergent Power*? (New York: Crane, Russak & Co., 1978), p. 67; William J. Barnds, "Comment," in John W. Mellor (ed.), *India: A Rising Middle Power* (Boulder, Colorado: Westview Press, 1979), pp. 180-88; and Norman D. Palmer, in *American Political Science Review*, vol. 72 (1978), p. 1177.

Indian Assertiveness as Middle Power

On the other hand, India as the preeminent power in the South Asian region would seem to have been a prime candidate for such containment in the early 1950s. For, the key characteristics of India's foreign policy behaviour then were: its refusal to align itself with the western bloc, its assertiveness on the global political scene as a non-aligned actor, its trenchant opposition to most American policies, and its implicit ambition to organise a bloc of the nonaligned countries outside the American sphere of influence. While India had already articulated the doctrine of nonalignment, it was only with the opening of the 1950s that it assumed an active role in international politics, and on the global level at that. With the Korean war, India began to play its international role with some finesse, holding itself forth as a self-appointed messenger for peace and as a self-assured mediator between the two superpowers. The Gandhian heritage of idealism and pacifism gave a tone of self-righteous moralising to Indian pronouncements, which grated the Americans, who arrogated to themselves the monopoly of international morality.

More significantly, India attempted to play a subject role in international politics even though it did not possess all the attributes necessary for such a role. In the process, it aroused the resentment and hostility of those whose own power and influence would as a consequence be diminished. At the same time, India endeavoured to overcome its power weakness by politically mobilising other Asian and African nations and by assuming, for a time, the leadership of the nonaligned nations. On a whole range of world issues -- Korea, China, Indochina, Southeast Asia, and the Japanese peace treaty -- India was especially assertive in opposition to the United States. This assertiveness in the first half of the 1950s, culminating in the Bandung conference, came at a time when the US was the sole subject in the international system and was determined to remain so. It is noteworthy that in congressional hearings in 1954, when Congressman Coudert asked, "Fundamentally does not that mean that the United States is undertaking to maintain for an indefinite period of years American dominance in the Far East?" Assistant Secretary of State Robertson laconically answered, "Yes, exactly."[2] Nehru protested at this presumption on the part of the United States, but it was in this frame of mind that American decisionmakers encountered Indian assertiveness in international politics.

As a result of its foreign policy posture, India came to be viewed by the United States not only as a continuous irritant but also as an inveterate claimant to an independent role in international politics. Dean Acheson was visibly incensed by Nehru's activities on the world scene; as one American scholar pointedly observed, "A permanent state of irritation is the best summary description of Acheson's attitude toward India."[3] John Foster Dulles characterised India's nonalignment not only as "an obsolete conception" but also as "an immoral and shortsighted conception."[4] Acheson did not publicly condemn India for its nonalignment, but Acheson's attitude was "indistinguishable from Dulles's."[5] Nonalignment became anathema to most Americans, and Nehru was dubbed an "aide and ally" of communism by American leaders like George Meany.[6]

[2] Cited in Coral Bell, *Survey of International Affairs 1954* (London: Oxford University Press, 1957), p. 284.

[3] Gaddis Smith, *Dean Acheson* (New York: Cooper Square Publishers, 1972), p. 375; see also Dean Acheson, *Present at the Creation* (New York: W.W. Norton and Co., 1969), pp. 334-36, 416-20.

[4] Michael A. Gulin, *John Foster Dulles: A Statesman and His Times* (New York: Columbia University Press, 1972), p. 259.

[5] Smith, *Dean Acheson*, p. 378.

[6] *New York Times*, December 14, 1955, p. 1; see also Durga Das, *India From Curzon to Nehru & After* (London: Wm. Collins, Sons and Co., 1969), p. 297.

India's policy was objectionable to the United States not only because it placed an obstacle in the way of American containment of the Soviet Union but also because it attempted to create an additional world force -- even though a force based not on military capabilities but on a political mobilisation of national elites in Asia and Africa. From the American perspective, India had arrogated to itself the privileges of a putative independent centre of power, thus contracting the American sphere of influence. As a consequence, India's position became unacceptable to the United States, notwithstanding the dedication of India's elites to democratic values, its establishment of a representative political system, its crushing of communist insurrections at home, and its membership of the Commonwealth.

Whether the United States was thus driven to a policy of containment, in part or in whole, of India as a rebellious middle power is, of course, a matter that ought to face the test, not simply of consistency with an analytical framework, but of evidence. However, when it comes to evidence on motivation in international relations it is no easy matter. For, in the struggle for power, nations must hide their real motives in order precisely to mislead adversaries, and even friends. Public declarations about the objectives of policies are thus a poor guide to real motives. Even classified documents do not fully reveal the motives of decision-makers, for such documents as the outcome of committee discussions or telephonic conversations tend often to austerely report what ought to be done, with such rationale as would cause the least harm if it were to become public. This concern over harm applies in relation not only to adversaries but also to the domestic legislature and the public. Interestingly, the fear of leaks is as pervasive in the United States as it is in Third World countries. Again, for strategic reasons or considerations of public relations, certain historical documents may be deliberately excluded from archival collections; thus, for example, the volume on "Iran, 1952-1954" in the FR series expunges all information on the US role in the 1953 coup in Iran.[7] The "smoking gun" in foreign relations is therefore not likely to be always readily available to clinch the resolution of a controversy, and consequently a considerable part of the case must rest on both logic and the totality of the evidence. Still, it will be widely accepted that private and classified information is more credible as evidence on motivation than are public statements.

An examination of the published official documentation for the period pertaining to the Republican administration prior to the announcement of the decision on military aid to Pakistan in February 1954 (FR 1952-1954, IX) does not, admittedly, reveal any special targeting of India for such military aid. However, that does not necessarily mean the inadequacy of the analytical framework but perhaps points to the limitation of the specific official documentation. That reservation is understandable in the light of the considerable sensitivity over the matter at the time, not only in relation to the bitter opposition to the move within India but also opposition from within the Congress. As a consequence, one has to go outside the official documentation in order to explore the matter of objectives beyond those simply relating to the containment of the Soviet Union.

The American Perception: Public and Private

An initial clue to the deficiency in official documentation is provided by perhaps the first analyst to study intensively the decision on military aid -- Selig Harrison. Having at one time served as correspondent for the Associated Press in South Asia, Harrison went on to write major scholarly works on the region and the Third World. In 1966, he pointedly underlined

[7] See the editorial, "History Bleached at State," *New York Times* (May 16, 1990), p. A26.

the two-pronged approach of American decision-makers on the question of objectives of the decision: one justification for public consumption, another for private information. As he put it:

> For the record John Foster Dulles defined the new military pact with Pakistan as part of the global collective-security pattern then being developed to meet an expected recurrence of conventional aggression by Communist ground forces throughout Asia. Off the record, Vice President Nixon defined the objectives of some elements in Washington *more candidly* in briefings with newsmen. Pakistan's readiness to enter into a military pact offered an opportunity, the Vice President felt, *to build a counterforce to Nehru's neutralism in the Indian leader's backyard*.[8]

As Vice President, Nixon himself was also an important participant in the decision, which followed a moving speech he made before the National Security Council after a wide-ranging tour through Asia. Indeed, Nixon is said to have been the star performer at the meeting of the Council. Curiously, though, the published FR documentation includes no reference to the role of Nixon in the decision. However, Nixon's admiring biographer, Ralph de Toledano, to whom Nixon opened his files, wrote in 1956, not long after the decision, that in that memorable speech before the National Security Council, Nixon expressed his feeling that "Nehru was contemptuous of flattery and respectful of strength," and forcefully urged military aid to Pakistan "as a counterforce to the confirmed neutralism of Jawaharlal Nehru's India." He further observed that Nixon was "convinced that India's

[8] Selig S. Harrison, "America, India, and Pakistan: A Chance for a Fresh Start," *Harper's*, No. 233 (July 1966), p. 67. Emphasis added.

neutralism was an outgrowth of the Prime Minister's belief that India could be a dominant force only if the rest of non-communist Asia were weak and unarmed."[9]

These revelations only confirmed what had already been apparent through highly credible reporting in the mass media. By October 1953 India had become aware of American plans to provide military aid to Pakistan, and when Nehru met with Nixon in New Delhi in December he devoted most of his two-hour talk with him to the isssue in an effort to dissuade the US from that course. The essence of his case was two-fold: American military aid would bring the cold war to South Asia; and Pakistan, through overconfidence as a result of the change in the military balance in the subcontinent, would likely resort to war. American Embassy officials told the Canadian High Commissioner in New Delhi, Escott Reid, that "Nixon had been impressed by the weight of these arguments." Apparently, Nixon left Nehru with the impression of a sympathetic hearing for his arguments.[10] But, if so, this was exactly the opposite of what Nixon's real intent was.

From New Delhi, Nixon went on to the then Pakistani capital of Karachi for a three-day visit. During that period, the respected *New York Times* correspondent Robert Trumbull cabled two despatches which laid bare American thinking; Nixon clearly was the source of these despatches even though their content was not specifically attributed to him. Trumbull's "informed sources" averred to him that it was about time to put "an end to Washington's patience with neutralism," of which Nehru was the chief proponent. It was their understanding that "Mr. Nehru's neutralist influence, which often has embarrassed the United States and its allies, would be lessened if an Asian power outspokenly opposed to

[9] Ralph de Toledano, *Nixon* (New York: Henry Holt, 1956), p. 164.

[10] Escott Reid, *Envoy to Nehru* (Delhi: Oxford University Press, 1981), p. 102.

Communism were to gain a position of greater prominence." The recommendation therefore was for the United States to assume "a position of greater independence in relation to the Indian Prime Minister."

There was further the sharp reminder of the basic opposition between the global power and the middle power: "His interests and what he believes to be India's interests may not be to the best interests of the United States and the United Nations." The fundamental question, however, related to influence; and here it was the other party that was charged with seeking undue influence, the argument being that Nehru "is not willing to allow any other government to be a pale rival to India in this area" through identifying India's own interests with Asia, the Middle East and Africa. It was felt that "India's diplomacy has been directed toward keeping her neighbours individually weak and divided among themselves, but internally stable and united under India's leadership." That is precisely what has given rise to India's conflict with the US: "*His major rival for influence in South Asia is the United States*. This explains his wary attitude toward Japan, Pakistan and other Asian countries on close terms with Washington."

The question therefore for Washington was to "determine whether India, a country often opposed to the United States in vital international dealings, is to obtain unquestioned dominance over this entire area, plus Africa, or is to remain merely the strongest individual power in an Asia-Arab-Africa bloc." A firmer course toward India was called for, and "an early practical step in that direction would be to strengthen the friendlier nations in this orbit, beginning with Pakistan." Nehru will, no doubt, protest, but "the basic reason for Mr. Nehru's opposition is that a stronger Pakistan, with all that this implies in the Moslem world, would threaten the dominance of India in Asia, the Near East, and Africa." A diplomacy based on power was then advocated towards Nehru: "He will be affected in his purposes by strength, decisive action and people who can say *'No' with power to back it up*. The United States must determine soon whether it is to the best interests of the free world to have India the only strong nation in this part of the world or to have a number of strong nations, with India stronger than the rest -- she merits that position if only because of her size -- but not dominant."[11]

Nothing could have expressed with any more brutal clarity the inherent conflict between the US as the hegemonic global power and India as the rebellious middle power, as also set out emphatically the means to be employed by the global power to counter middle power pretensions to greater influence in the region. The stance taken by Nixon, however, was apparently no less true of the Republican Secretary of State, John Foster Dulles. Chester Bowles, who served as American Ambassador to India part way into the Eisenhower administration as a carry-over from his previous posting under the Truman administration, subsequently wrote: "Soon stories began to appear of behind-the-scenes manoeuvering within the State Department and Pentagon for a review of the earlier negative decision. Of particular concern was the report that Secretary of State Dulles, exasperated by Nehru's refusal to sign the Japanese Peace Treaty that he (Dulles) had negotiated or to modify India's nonaligned foreign policies, was in favour of the proposed buildup of the Pakistan military."[12]

That such views were not strictly restricted to Nixon or Dulles, nor that they were simply confined to an attempt at containment, becomes obvious from the memoirs of the Canadian High Commissioner in New Delhi at the time, Escott Reid. Within days of the Nixon visit, an American official, presumably the CIA station chief in New Delhi, met with Reid at the former's request -- since they knew each

[11] *Ibid.*, pp. 102-103; and *New York Times*, December 9 and 10, 1953.

[12] Chester Bowles, *Promises to Keep: My Years in Public Life 1941-1969* (New York: Harper & Row, 1971), p. 478.

other, having spent time together at Oxford in the 1920s – and gave him an insight into the larger American design on the military aid question. The argument of the CIA official was, in Reid's words, as follows:

> India was the only possible source of a mass army for the West in a third world war. A military agreement between the United States and Pakistan would isolate India. India would find that it would not be able to build up its armaments to match the increase in Pakistan's because the United States would put pressure on Britain not to provide arms, and would also see to it that India did not receive other essential imports from western countries.... These developments would weaken Nehru and the Congress Party and strengthen the right-wing Hindu group, the Jana Sangh, some of whose members were prepared to support a military agreement with the United States. The objective of the United States in making a military agreement with Pakistan was thus to put India in a position where it had no recourse but to make a military agreement with the United States which would ultimately lead to India becoming an ally of the United States, and the source of a mass army for the West in a third world war.[13]

In this fashion, the US sought through the policy of containment a more effective satellisation of India. Reid went on to note that "the threat which was conveyed to me in this conversation that the United States might cut off essential supplies to India if India refused to enter into a military aid agreement was taken seriously by the business community in India." The Indians evinced fear that even the export of

[13] Reid, pp. 103-104.

trucks to India would be disallowed; the head of Ford of Canada's subsidiary sought Reid's intervention to assure the Indian government that Ford of Canada stood on a separate basis than its American parent and "could therefore pursue a different policy on the provision of trucks to India than Ford in the United States."[14] Again, at a lunch at the American Embassy in January 1954, the Canadian High Commissioner found the American Ambassador and his deputy pressing a British guest with access to high Indian officials "to answer the question whether the effect of large American military aid to Pakistan would not be that India would itself request military aid from the United States. Their tenacity in pressing this question confirmed my feeling that this was indeed the hope held by important groups in the American administration."[15]

Apparently cognisant of the administration's thinking, Senator Fulbright quite aptly warned that the military pact with Pakistan was basically an anti-Nehru tactic "designed to force his hand."[16] It becomes obvious then that the aim of American military aid to Pakistan was not simply some containment of the Soviet Union, or collective defence in the Middle East, but also had India specifically as its target. Nehru was thus not wrong in his perception that American decision-makers "imagine that an alliance between Pakistan and the US would bring such overwhelming pressure on India as to compel her to change her policy of nonalignment."[17] Interestingly, American Ambassador George Allen, within less than a month after the decision on military aid, directly linked it to the intended setbacks to Nehru and his foreign policy; in a secret cable to Washington, he stated:

[14] *Ibid.*

[15] *Ibid.*, p. 105.

[16] Selig S. Harrison, "India, Pakistan and the U.S.–II," *New Republic*, No. 141 (August 24, 1959), p. 21.

[17] Kuldip Nayar, *India After Nehru* (Delhi: Vikas Publications, 1975), p. 52.

> This decision has been *serious defeat for Nehru*. I hope with time *it will undermine his entire concept of neutralism in this region*. If this develops *it will be a major victory for US policy*. We should try to find way in which price we pay for such victory is cut to minimum. The price might well be permanent impairment of Indian-American relations and alienation of Indian good will for indefinite period.... I know the vigour with which those who find Nehru exasperating will argue that we should not cater to him in any way. I believe, however, that we may well let our own feelings do us a disservice if we fail to look beyond the present.(FR 1952-1954, XI, 1350-52; emphasis added)

All the American ambassadors in South Asia and its neighbouring areas shared the sentiment that military aid to Pakistan and its linkage with Middle East would be beneficial to the US in that it would weaken neutralism and strengthen those forces which wish to align with the West.(Ibid., 1118-20)

The link between the decision on military aid and motives specifically relating to India is clear from the evidence, even if much of it is not from official sources. However, one does not have to rely simply on verbal testimony to discern the intentions of US decision-makers. Equally important is the actual pattern of state behaviour of the United States. Here, it is noteworthy that the weapons-mix of military aid provided to Pakistan left no doubt that it was directed at India. The Indian government brought this to the attention of the United States, but to no avail. As Bowles stated:

> The Indian Government pointed out that the military equipment that we were giving to Pakistan had no relevance to our alleged military objectives. If the Pakistan Army were actually designed to become part of a United States-sponsored defence system to

> discourage a Soviet or Chinese military movement through the Himalayas or the Hindu Kush Mountains, it would be seeking equipment appropriate for fighting in the mountain areas. However, the equipment we supplied Pakistan – tanks, motorised artillery and the like -- was suitable for use only on a relatively flat terrain, in other words, on the plains of North India. Moreover, from the outset, the Pakistan Government had itself made clear that it had no quarrel with either the USSR or China and privately admitted that its military build-up was, in fact, directed against India.[18]

Beyond the verbal evidence and actual state behaviour of the US, a more adequate appreciation of American motives in the decision requires an understanding of attitude formation that preceded the Eisenhower administration.

[18] Bowles, p. 480.

Chapter Three
The Intellectual Heritage from the Truman Administration

It has often been thought that there was a vital difference between alliances under the Truman/Acheson dispensation, which were focussed on centres of industrial power and countries with which the US shared a community of interest, and the Eishenhower/Dulles alliances which were oriented to countries that did not share these characteristics.[1] If there was, indeed, a difference between the two types of alliances, it was less conceptual than chronological, for the Truman administration itself had endeavoured to build a Middle East Defence Organisation, which foundered only on the opposition of Egypt as the middle power of that region. More pertinently, while the US-Pakistan military alliance became effective in 1954 under a Republican administration, the proposal itself was of much earlier origin; as the historian on Acheson commented: "John Foster Dulles was then Secretary of State, but he was carrying out a policy that had been initiated by Acheson."[2] Another scholar agrees: "In fairness to Dulles it should be emphasised that he only carried to their logical or illogical conclusion the policies in regard to Pakistan that had been conceived by the national security apparatus during the Democratic Administration of Harry S. Truman."[3]

[1] Terry L. Diebel and John Lewis Gaddis (ed.), *Containing the Soviet Union: A Critique of US Policy* (Washington, D.C.: Pergamon-Brassey's International Defence Publishers, 1987), pp. 100-119.

[2] Gaddis Smith, *Dean Acheson* (New York: Cooper Square Publishers, 1972), p. 377.

[3] M. S. Venkataramani, *The American Role in Pakistan* (New Delhi: Radiant Publishers, 1983), p. 202.

Nor should the Republican administration be considered as marking a complete break in policy more generally from the earlier Democratic administration. That it differed more in its rhetoric than in actual policy in many areas is widely acknowledged.[4] But there was also continuity in personnel as well. Eisenhower had not too long before been the supreme commander of the NATO forces in Europe, and at one time it was not certain whether he wished to run on the Democratic or Republican ticket. Dulles, who became Secretary of State, had been placed in charge of the Japanese peace treaty negotiations by none other than Acheson himself. Henry A. Byroade was appointed Assistant Secretary of State for Near Eastern, South Asian and African Affairs in April 1952, and continued to function in that position through 1954. It should not therefore occasion surprise if there should be continuity in thinking at the cabinet level of the State Department. Indeed, it can be safely asserted that a similar mindset had come to be shared by the two administrations in relation to the geopolitics of the region. The evolution of that mindset has to be seen in the context of the region's geopolitical structure.

South Asian Geopolitics and Initial American Posture

The withdrawal of British power from South Asia in 1947 left behind a changed geopolitical structure in the subcontinent. The natural features of the subcontinent have made it into a single geopolitical fortress, bounded by high walls in the north in the shape of the Himalayas and a vast moat in the south in the form of the Indian Ocean and its extensions. However, it was not until British colonial dominion that a single central political authority, through

[4] John Lewis Gaddis, *Stategies of Containment: A Critical Appraisal of Postwar American National Security Policy* (New York: Oxford University Press, 1982), p. 152.

direct and indirect rule, coincided with the geographic limits of the region. The colonial rulers undergirded the security of the subcontinent with a policy of the "reverse slopes" under which no external power was to be allowed to have a presence on the southern side of the "iron fence" of the Himalayas. Not only that, this policy was further supplemented by a policy of "buffer states" around India in Tibet, Afghanistan and Iran so that external major powers would not even have a presence immediately on the other side of the Himalayas either. With the end of colonial rule, however, came the end of the buffer arrangements. Further, with it also collapsed the single central authority. The partition of the subcontinent resulted in two major states, India and Pakistan, with the former preeminent in political power, being some four times the size of the latter's population and territory.

What potential possibilities in terms of strategic cooperation did the new geopolitical structure open to the new hegemonic global power, risen as a successor to the British empire? It would seem there were two basic options, depending on the behaviour of the middle power. From Washington's perspective the ideal arrangement would be a cooperative middle power, managing a cooperative region, possibly under a regional organisation. If the region as a whole was not cooperative, the middle power could even be assisted in managing it through resource transfers. On the other hand, if the middle power were not cooperative, but was indeed rebellious, then a regional organisation under the leadership of the middle power – even if it were possible – which barred access of the global power to the region, would be unacceptable. More to the point, the new geopolitical structure had exposed the middle power's "institutionalised vulnerability" in the form of Pakistan, which could be exploited as an instrument for purposes of containment and modification of the behaviour of the middle power.

Indeed, several features of Pakistan appeared to fit it admirably for the role of a local counterweight against India.

First, Pakistan was itself a substantial power; the equal of France and Germany combined in size, it would have been a middle power in its own right were it not for the fact of its being lodged in the neighbourhood of India, China and the Soviet Union. Second, hostility towards India was a natural condition for Pakistan, given its religion-based statehood. Thirdly, and relatedly, because of its natural affinity with the Muslim states of the Middle East, Pakistan could call into play a larger religion-based alliance against India. Because of their own apprehensions about India's power, even minor powers of the subcontinent may well collaborate with Pakistan in this endeavour. In this situation, what strategies Washington would adopt would fundamentally depend on the behaviour of India, as the regional power, towards the US.

At the birth of the two nations of India and Pakistan in 1947, Washington was not certain of their future foreign policy orientation, and was consequently inclined to be evenhanded in its relationship with them. Besides, with China still outside the Soviet bloc, it did not consider the area to be of any particular strategic value. Still, it seemed to place a higher strategic value on the real estate in Pakistan because of its proximity to the Middle East. Moreover, the United States initially tended to defer to the authority and expertise of Great Britain, with its earlier imperial and present Commonwealth connection with the area. Gradually, however, after a period of transition the US was to take over Britain's role as security manager of the subcontinent, much as it had done earlier in Greece and Turkey in the wake of the decline of British power; any resentment on the part of the British was then simply brushed aside.

As late as 1949, the US continued to have largely a non-discriminatory posture toward the chief countries of the subcontinent, and was indeed anxious to work out a regional cooperative arrangement among them, even as it recognised India's primary role in the region. Indicative of such a posture was the top secret report of a subcommittee of the

State-Army-War-Navy-Air Force Coordinating Committee (SANACC) of April 19, 1949.(FR 1949, VI, 8-31) Although the region was not considered to be of any particular strategic value to the US in military terms – barring the Karachi-Lahore area which may be of use for air bases – it was nonetheless a basic strategic objective of the US to prevent encroachment by the Soviet Union in the region as that "would endanger our national policy of Communist containment"; besides, the loss of access to the area's manpower, raw materials and productive capacity "would gravely affect the security of the US." However, it considered it "unrealistic to propose the necessary strengthening of the armed forces" of the chief countries of the region, because of the strained relations between them and because of other existing commitments of the US and UK.

The United States was not ready at the time to make any commitment to possible military action either, but was nonetheless eager to develop "a cooperative attitude" in the countries of the region so as to obtain military bases. The SANACC subcommittee felt encouraged not only by many of the educated classes having studied in the US, but also by the fact that the US would likely be the only source of capital goods and military equipment for the region: "In the military sphere the principal armies of South Asia are now equipped largely with British and US material...and so long as they remain dependent upon us for their continuing requirements it is unlikely that they would or could turn against us." Continued consultation with the British on supply of arms to the region was still felt necessary.

Significantly, the SANACC subcommittee wanted to encourage cooperation in the region, asking that any American assistance for the area "should be utilised as far as practicable as an instrument to effect cooperation within the region." At the time, it considered it to be self-defeating to provide assistance to any one country, which would result in the alienation of others. It therefore urged that "a regional approach is necessary" in any aid programme, recognising at the same time that "India is the natural political and economic centre of South Asia and aid given to the peripheral countries would have to be adapted to conditions in India." Such regional cooperation had, however, to be guided along constructive lines.

The subcommittee's approach to Indian activism in Asian affairs at the time was shrewdly mild and indulgent. It saw the Asian conference on Indonesia held in New Delhi in January 1949 as possibly leading to an Asian bloc, but one that was likely to be exploited by Moscow and to aggravate racial tensions between the Orient and Occident. However, it cautioned against efforts to undercut its formation, since they "would probably be ineffective and would certainly intensify anti-US sentiment in Asia. Our efforts would be more fruitful if directed toward impressing upon India, now in the leading position, and the other Asian nations the importance of acting within the framework of the UN and of avoiding immoderate emphasis on alleged racial issues."

Interestingly, in mid-1949, the Policy Planning Staff at State, studied the possibility of a regional organisation in the Middle East on the model of NATO, and considered the issue of the countries that ought to be included in such an organisation. It felt that the inclusion of India in a Middle East regional pact would result in a "too large and unwieldy" organisation, while "it would be unrealistic to include Afghanistan and Pakistan without India since the usefulness for security purposes of Afghanistan and Pakistan depends very largely on the facilities in depth to be found in India." It went on to suggest the formation of two regional groups, one each for the Middle East and South Asia, with Iran a member of both.(Ibid., 31-39)

The Perception of Rivalry and Containment

By 1950, however, the differing policy orientations of India and Pakistan had become crystallised in American eyes and there was considerable rethinking in Washington, not so much on how to organise a regional association in South Asia, but on how to use the existing political differences in the subcontinent against India. On a variety of issues, India had come to feature strong differences with the US -- recognition of China and its admission to UN, Korean war, Indochina and, more generally, "power politics" and military pacts. As a secret Department of State Policy Statement of December 1, 1950 was to acknowledge: "Divergencies between United States and Indian views toward China and Indochina are serious foreign policy conflicts blocking closer understanding with India."(FR 1950, V, 1480) India was, no doubt, playing an important role, but not one to American advantage. The consequent deterioration in their mutual relations caused concern even to the British, who urged obtaining India's support in future US plans. Despite the annoyance with India's activities, there was still some ambivalence in the American attitude. Assistant Secretary of State George McGhee averred that "the US fully recognised the importance of having India's cooperation" but that "our different interpretations of events in Asia constituted a running sore." The US contemplated more effective consultation with India in the future, but thought there were likely to be many obstacles.(Ibid., 202-203)

By this time, Washington had significantly also come to develop doubts about Indian power ambitions, particularly in the area of nuclear energy. A memorandum prepared in the office of Under Secretary of State Lovett in late 1948 for briefing newly-appointed American Ambassador to India, Loy W. Henderson, noted: "The aspirations of Indian officials in atomic energy development appear illimitable." Even as the US wanted monazite and beryl from India for its own use, it was against helping India in exchange with the latter's nuclear energy programme. Even the local processing of atomic raw materials in India was not acceptable to the US. The United States "ruled out" any assistance to India in the establishment of a beryllia processing plant. Instead, more generally, it decided, in order to advance "disenchantment" in India about nuclear energy, that "the Indian officials be given frank appraisal of the difficulties ahead in their ambitions toward atomic energy development."(FR 1948, I, 758-65)

As against the difficulties with India, Washington saw Pakistan as visibly more friendly and cooperative. There was recognition within the administration of the essential difference between the two local powers, with McGhee underlining "the Korean issue as one instance" of Pakistan's useful influence; accordingly, "the US was inclined to welcome Pakistani initiative in the Moslem world."(FR 1950, V, 204) For its part, Pakistan left US officials in no doubt as to the purposes for which it was undertaking such an initiative. When McGhee had met with Finance Minister Ghulam Mohammed in Karachi in December 1949, the latter had told him how a bloc of nations organised on the basis of Islam could be of importance to the US in checking Soviet territorial expansion. More importantly, however, "again and again he reverted to the importance of the fight which Pakistan was making for independence, both political and economic, and *insisted the new Middle East grouping was essential in Pakistan's fight with India*."[5] Of this and other meetings with Pakistani officials, McGhee was to note later in his memoirs that "Pakistan, particularly because of the pressure of its rivalry with India, was courting us assiduously. In seeking aid, particularly arms aid, Pakistan took pains to dissociate itself from Indian neutralism."[6] Indeed, the US had

[5] Rajendra K. Jain (ed.), *US-South Asian Relations, 1947-1982* (New Delhi: Radiant Publishers, 1983), II, p. 25; emphasis added.

[6] George McGhee, *Envoy to the Middle World: Adventures in*

already begun to recognise Pakistan's intent, and found it to be of possible advantage to the US. In September 1949, in a memorandum to Ambassador-at-Large Phillip C. Jessup, the Deputy Assistant Secretary of State, Raymond A. Hare, had observed:

> Pakistan's endeavour to assume the leadership of a Middle East Muslim bloc is to create a counter force to what it believes to be the "Hindu imperialism" of the new Indian Republic. India has emerged from World War II as the strongest power in Asia. Its position of dominance will probably increase as its power potential is developed. We have *no great assurance that India in the future will ally itself with us* and we have some reason to believe that it might not. Pakistan, if given reasonable encouragement, might prove the more reliable friend. In certain circumstances, therefore, *a strong Muslim bloc under Pakistan leadership could provide a very desirable balance of power in Asia*. Until we know more about how the future alignment of power is to be shaped, therefore, we should take no action which would indicate that we do not favour Pakistan's endeavour to form a Muslim bloc.[7]

The following year there was more authoritative recognition of the advantage to the US of Pakistan in a secret Department of State Policy Statement of April 3, 1950. More significantly, this advantage had now become transformed: from Pakistan as a possible ally to Pakistan as a countervailing power available for use by the US, specifically directed against Indian ambition, quite independent of any Soviet containment. Even though the statement added a qualification at the end, by

Diplomacy (New York: Harper & Row, 1983), p. 92.

[7] Jain, p. 23. See also Venkataramani, pp. 96-97.

paying the customary homage to the virtues of regional cooperation in South Asia to meet the Soviet threat, it underlined with brutal clarity its central intent, should India prove unbending before American desires:

> the development of a Pakistan-India *entente cordiale* appears remote. Moreover, the vigour and methods which have characterised India's execution of its policy of consolidating the princely states, and its inflexible attitude with regard to Kashmir, may indicate national traits which in time, if not controlled, could make India Japan's successor in Asiatic imperialism. In such a circumstance *a strong Muslim bloc under the leadership of Pakistan, and friendly to the US, might afford a desirable balance of power in South Asia.* On the other hand our interests should be better served by cooperation than by rivalry between India and Pakistan as long as Soviet expansionism threatens South Asia.(FR 1950, V, 1499; emphasis added)

Notwithstanding the underlying realpolitik intent aimed against India, the United States was not yet ready to take such irreversible action as would alienate India. Apart from contemplating more effective consultation, the US sought regional stability in South Asia. Without the traditional deference to Great Britain's responsibilities in the region, it took a more direct hand in counselling India and Pakistan about the wisdom of averting war, to which the two countries were inching. Even though favouring Pakistan on the Kashmir dispute, partly by operating through Great Britain, the US endeavoured to retain the semblance of neutrality. Further, it contemplated putting together an economic aid programme for South Asia, believing that "countries in such close proximity to the USSR orbit need the stiffening and confidence provided by the United States economic assistance."(FR 1950,

V, 169)

Washington still entertained the hope that India and Pakistan could work together. It saw merit in a regional association; but one sort was not acceptable even though the US could look at the situation with a degree of equanimity (since it was not likely to come into existence), while the other was not possible on the rocks of local rivalry:

> The region suspects the West European nations and the United States of attempting to maintain an imperialist position in Asia and of discriminating against non-white peoples. Thus, India, which is discreetly eager to head a South and Southeast Asian regional association, regards the natural bases of such an association as anti-colonialism and neutrality in the cold war. There is little immediate prospect that a regional association will develop in South and Southeast Asia. Ceylon and Nepal fear India's size and potential power, and would be reluctant to enter into regional arrangements which might pave the way for Indian domination of the region. Pakistan is unwilling to accept a position subordinate to India and seeks to counter-balance India's greater strength by developing close relations with its Moslem neighbours to the West.(Top Secret "Regional Policy Statement: South Asia," October 9, 1950; FR 1950, V, 245-54)

Up to this point, the US had counted on the inner dynamics of the region to block India; soon, however, it would be ready to add its own weight toward the same end.

A series of developments were to exacerbate relations between the US and India, and strengthen American determination to proceed with its plans in South Asia with less regard for India's sensibilities. On the one hand, these included the intensification of the Cold War, with the two blocs actually locked in physical combat in a limited war in Korea, and the increasing shakiness of the western position in the Middle East, especially in Iran. On the other hand, they were accompanied by India's opposition to the American extension of the Korean war beyond the 38th parallel, to American plans for the Japanese peace treaty with the projected signing of a security treaty before Japan actually became an independent state, and to the American-sponsored "Uniting for Peace" resolution (which sought to circumvent Soviet veto in the Security Council by endowing the then US-dominated UN General Assembly with broader jurisdiction). These developments brought in their train a chain of consequences for the region of South Asia. Already, in January 1951, President Truman had approved NSC 98/1, which noted: "The time has come to pursue our objectives with more vigour. We are now in a position to assess the attitudes and policies of area governments as well as the possibilities and limitations of our influence. Moreover, the fall of China and the threat to Indo-China and the balance of Southeast Asia has given added urgency to the achievement of our objectives in this region. *We must henceforth more frequently accept calculated risks in attacking the problems of South Asia.*"[8]

As if to suggest the precise lines for such follow-up action, a five-day South Asian Regional Conference of United States Diplomatic and Consular Officers from the Departments of State and Defence, CIA, US embassies in South Asia and neighbouring countries was held in Ceylon in early 1951 under the chairmanship of Assistant Secretary of State McGhee. The conference underscored the sharpness with which the US now evaluated India and Pakistan differentially from the perspective of its interests.(FR 1951, VI, 1664-88) American concerns came to centre on India, as the leader of a neutral bloc, constituting a rival to the US for influence in Asia. It

[8] Jain, p. 44.

was Indian influence per se that was at issue, not India as some proxy for the Soviet Union, for as late as May 1953, Nehru was telling Dulles "India has almost no contacts, economic or political, with the Government of Soviet Russia."(FR 1952-1954, IX, 115-17) If India moved closer to the Soviet Union subsequently it was in reaction to US policy which India perceived as aimed against it.

The conference was convinced that India's foreign policy rested on a "fallacious basis" and constituted a danger to both Asia and world peace, while its attempt to organise a neutral third force through attacks on the West suggest that "it partially follows the Cominform line." The conference counselled "a policy of patience built on firmness" towards India even as it asked that the US "should challenge it vigorously, both at home and abroad," if it affected collective security.

Normally, the US had featured enthusiasm for regional organisations, but its attitude towards South Asia was entirely different now on account of its distrust of India's possible role as rival to the US for influence:

> In view of India's ambitions for political hegemony, its advocacy of a doctrine of appeasement, and its tendencies toward abandoning support of the principle of collective security, the United States *should not at this time encourage the formation of a South Asian regional bloc, since such an organisation might come under India's domination*.

Again, it warned: "we should refrain from action in the United Nations which would assist in promoting a regional organisation in South Asia, which *would probably come under Indian domination*." Further, while noting that India believes the United Nations to be under American domination and control for the promotion of US interests, it recommended:

> Every effort should be made to guard against the division of the United Nations into opposing Asian and Western blocs. Specifically we should *be more active in opposing Nehru's efforts to create a neutral bloc* among the Asian and Arab states.

On the other hand, the conference still thought India to be "a worthwile long-term risk from a military standpoint," and asked for non-pressure methods to win its friendship and support. It was, however, dubious about India providing military assistance to "the free world" in the event of war, but nonetheless thought that an offer of military "aid to India, and acceptance of similar aid by Pakistan, might spark a change in Indian policy and provide a stimulus which in the long term would bring great benefits to the free world from India's military potential, raw materials, industrial output, manpower, and communications facilities." It further felt that use of India as a production base for military supplies may be "one of the best means of securing *India's ultimate alignment with the West.*" (FR 1951, VI, 1664-88; emphases added)

As for Pakistan, the conference believed that its "present orientation to the West" and the possibility of its supplying ground forces required that "the United States military authorities should consider on *an urgent basis* the desirability of the United States entering into an early understanding with Pakistan, which would provide for equipping and building up Pakistan's military forces." Although it wanted Pakistan to be a member in a possible Middle East military pact, the conference urged that "*such action, however, should not delay the understanding with Pakistan.*" (FR 1951, VI, 1667; emphasis added) In this manner, the conference made it clearly manifest that the military build-up of Pakistan stood on a completely independent basis rather than necessarily linked with defence of the Middle East. At the same time, American Ambassador to Pakistan, Avra Warren, informed the conference that "the most significant factor in the political life of Pakistan was its obsession with India."[9]

An extremely useful insight into the urgency for building up Pakistan militarily, even without a Middle East pact, is provided by a secret briefing paper entitled "Means to Combat India's Policy of Neutralism," prepared by the Department of State for the meetings of the Foreign Ministers of the United States, United Kingdom and France, held in Washington in September 1951.(FR 1951, VI, 2172-74) The paper's title and the targeted audience is fully revealing both of the escalating American obsession with Indian foreign policy and of the American perception of the depth of opposition between India and US in their rivalry for influence in Asia. The State Department took India's foreign policy of "neutralism" as militating against collective security and "therefore, in final analysis, is favourable to the Soviet Union," with India's refusal to sign the Japanese peace treaty serving as only "the latest manifestation" of such neutralism.

The State Department believed that, although Nehru knew that India's interests lay with the West, he refused to join with it unequivocally for fear that such action would "put India in a subordinate position vis-a-vis the US and the UK, and limit thereby India's ability to play a pivotal role in Asian affairs." For its part, State was afraid that other Asian states may come to appreciate the rationale for "neutralism" even though they themselves may not possess India's strengths against possible subversion or attack. More important, however, was the revelation in the briefing paper -- with astonishing explicitness -- as to how the US viewed its military aid as serving as an instrument to cut India's role and influence:

> In the long run an effective means of combatting "neutralism" lies in *increasing the capacity of other non-Communist Asian states to exert influence and leadership* in building collective security. *Success in*

[9] McGhee, p. 281.

> *this objective would presumably result in a commensurate limitation on the ability of Mr. Nehru to maintain India as the pivotal Asian state* between what he regards as the "two power blocs." *This objective is in part the basis of the economic and military assistance which the United States is currently giving* various Asian countries.(Ibid.; emphasis added)

If this were so, what could be more effective than giving military aid to Pakistan in Nehru's own backyard! A Middle East pact may be desirable for the same purpose, but was not essential to it.

An intellectual underpinning to the American strategy for containing India through military aid to its local rivals was provided by the American Ambassador to India, Loy Henderson. The ambassador was no stranger to containment, having been the US official to receive the British request to the US in 1947 to assume the burden of protecting Greece and Turkey, and also to see it as symbolic of the larger imperial decline of Great Britain.[10] In a long telegram, reminiscent of Kennan's on the Soviet Union, Henderson on September 6, 1951 sought to explain to Washington India's rejection of the Japanese peace treaty and to predict future Indian state behaviour.(FR 1951, VI, 2179-81) He rejected any notion of India's stand on the treaty being merely a reflection of the current state of India-US relations. Rather, in abbreviated telegraphic language, he sought to place it in the context of the general framework of Nehru's thinking on foreign policy, seeing it as representing a "logical step on part Nehru in his efforts attain one his primary fon policy objectives, that is, eventual exclusion from mainland and waters Asia all Western

[10] Deborah Welch Larson, *Origins of Containment: A Psychological Explanation* (Princeton: Princeton University Press, 1985), pp. 241-42, 303-304.

milit power and what he wld consider as Western polit and econ pressures." In this manner, Henderson saw a grand design or master plan at work in Nehru's -- deliberately differentiating between Nehru and India -- foreign policies, under which Nehru sought to detach China from the Soviet bloc and Japan from the American alliance. The underlying immediate goal of Nehru's in this plan was taken to be the formation of a common front with these two Asian giants under the slogan of "Asian nationalism" in his bid for "attainment united Asia in which he can play important role....and which he wld like use in pursuing further objectives." Henderson understood the content of this "Asian nationalism" to be a combination of "Asia for Asians" and "anti-Westernism."

Although Nehru had not succeeded in having China abandon the Sino-Soviet alliance to enter into a partnership with India, for Henderson he had, through the rejection of the Japanese peace treaty, "laid basis which will enable him carry on subsequent campaign stimulate and gain influence over nationalistic and anti-white elements in Jap." Henderson suspected that

> In carrying on his campaign to attain his objectives in Asia Nehru not likely move too openly or rapidly. He will not wish arouse too much hostility or indignation in US. He realises for some time to come Ind will sorely need certain capital and consumption goods which only US can furnish. He not likely disclose his real objectives. He will probably continue try appear as democratic idealist primarily interested in welfare downtrodden masses of Asia; as David who regretfully faces materialistic and clumsy Goliath of militarism and imperialism.... He will continue make special effort charm and flatter naive Amer and Brit, who he thinks might be useful in helping mould public opinion in his favour

> or in supporting policies in their countries which wld facilitate gaining of his fon policy objectives. He will continue make minor concessions and friendly gestures from time to time to US in order keep down tide resentment and make US officials think, "He will come to our side eventually if we are patient and handle him properly." He not likely, however, change his basic policies....

Perhaps unwittingly, Henderson elevated the conflict between the US and India to the status of a titanic struggle between a virtuous western Goliath and a scheming Oriental David, with the latter thus not only fit for an application of the policy of containment, but one for which a ready intellectual rationale was available in justification. Interestingly, an authority well versed in containment, American Ambassador Kirk in Moscow, cabled Acheson that he had found Henderson's telegram to be of great interest, "providing clearest exposition Nehru character and programme to date."(Ibid.) To Henderson's credit, at the end he warned the US against "playing into hands our enemies if in endeavouring meet Nehru's campaign against US in Asia we shld 'write India off' or take measures likely wound sensibilities of Ind people."

At Nehru's farewell luncheon for him, Henderson expounded -- on Washington's instructions to remind Nehru of "possible consequences to India if GOI fols present course in fon relations" -- his views on India attempting to draw Japan away from the US, which would mean "it would be fallacious for either US or India believe our differences were merely superficial." Nehru tried to disabuse him of any such notion, averring that the idea was "novel" to him, that the thought of it had not occurred to him, and that he could not imagine anyone figuring he had such a policy. He rejected the whole line of thought as "erroneous."(FR 1951, VI, 2182-85)

Although the view on the framework of Nehru's foreign policy may initially have been Henderson's personal one, it was subsequently more generally accepted in the administration. After the transfer of power to the Republican administration, a secret National Security Council study around the time of military aid to Pakistan in February 1954, not only referred to Nehru's "dreams of making India a great power" and "dreams of South Asia, under his leadership, rising to become a great 'third force' in the world," but asserted: "India would like to separate Japan from its close association with the United States."(FR 1952-1954, XI, 1096-1117)

It is apparent from the review of Washington's changing orientation toward India that India was seen -- howsoever unrealistically -- as a serious rival for influence, and therefore deserving of containment. This view had become quite pervasive throughout the establishment. It is precisely this perceptual universe that Nixon and Dulles shared; their views, as described earlier -- though not revealed in the official record -- were not an aberration but an accurate manifestation of that universe. Any path analysis of the decision on military aid to Pakistan, which is narrowly restricted to that decision alone, is likely to prove inadequate in uncovering motivation insofar as it ignores the attitudinal complex that had come to prevail in Washington's decision-making machinery. Incidentally, that complex can be taken to have been shared by the Congress as well; when Ambassador Bowles suggested a larger economic aid package for India, Acheson refused to touch it on the ground that "there would be a massacre if the administration went to the Congress with such a request."[11] The administration's earlier problems with Congress in obtaining food aid for famine relief in India were indicative of the sentiment in Congress.

[11] Smith, p. 378.

Favouring the Local Counterweight

In contrast to its perspective on India, the United States had come to be keenly appreciative of Pakistan's orientation to the West; as the secret Department of State Policy Statement of July 1, 1951 on Pakistan noted: "Pakistan does not suffer from the violent anti-Westernism and deep-rooted neutrality that prevents India from cooperating fully with the US and its allies."(FR 1951, VI, 2206-16) The United States was then eager to develop a military relationship with it to counter, even if only in part, India's neutralism. If that was so, Pakistan for its own reasons pursued the procurement of military supplies from the US with amazing tenacity and success.

Within a single month in late 1951 a Pakistani delegation met four times separately with Assistant Secretary of State McGhee, Director of South Asian Affairs Donald Kennedy and Secretary of State Acheson who, in addition, conferred with Pakistani Foreign Minister Zafrullah Khan, all to obtain "as much military equipment" as Pakistan could and "to receive it as a gift, under a loan arrangement, or by outright purchase." The delegation told McGhee: "Now Pakistan was taking the initiative and putting forth its requirements. It was also ready to hear what the US wanted of Pakistan." The delegation also obliquely suggested that the target for the arms was "to fight for Kashmir." When questioned by Kennedy about cooperation in Middle East defence, it stated: "US knows what it can do and so does Pakistan. Each country knows what it wants. The time was past for words; Pakistan wanted action." Acheson assured the delegation of "very sympathetic consideration," while the latter expressed interest in Middle East defence. Khan went further and told Acheson that Pakistan would want its relations with the West "to be very close and not through some loose arrangements" as were being contemplated for the Middle East.(FR 1951, VI, 2220-29) The US then acted rather promptly on several requests for military sales, indicative of the increasingly close relations developing between the two countries, but no decision was in sight yet on the kind of intimate relationship that Zafrullah Khan sought.

Meanwhile, the United States began to assume not only a more active and interventionist role, as befit a global power, in subcontinental disputes like Kashmir but also a decidedly pro-Pakistani stance, notwithstanding its straining to give the appearance of impartiality. There were close and frequent consultations with Pakistan about moves in the UN over Kashmir, while India was rebuffed, and there was even violation of the trust that customarily went with the appointment of Americans to UN positions. The Indians suspected American partisanship as a way of "getting back" at India for its foreign policy in Korea and the Far East, as well as an advance payment for a future military relationship with Pakistan. But they could not possibly have known of the extent to which the highly respected American mediator for the UN on Kashmir, Frank Graham, received and sought American official advice before formulating his recommendations on Kashmir while working under UN auspices, and equally of his endeavours for mobilisation by the US government of newspaper editorial support in the US in order to gain greater leverage for him in India.(FR 1951, VI, 1699-1928)[12]

True, the American partisanship on behalf of Pakistan would intensify even more after the latter had become a military ally, and the Truman administration was not yet willing to identify itself completely with Pakistan's position, but it had pushed India's alienation to great lengths. Shrewdly, the US worked closely with the UK on Kashmir in

[12] See esp. pp. 1717, 1729, 1736, 1738-39, 1776-77, 1819, 1821, 1825, 1835, 1839, 1842, 1844, 1845-449, 1859, 1862, 1869-73, 1875-78, 1882-83, 1886-87, 1888, 1890-96, 1902, 1905, 1911-16, 1919-20, 1923-24.

an attempt to diffuse Indian resentment. At times, but not always, the UK was unwilling to align itself fully with the US on the issue for fear of driving India into a withdrawal from the Commonwealth; the private American reaction to this was, as expressed by Acting Assistant Secretary of State Burton Berry, one of disdainful condemnation: "they do not necessarily look with favour on any increase in our activities or influence in South Asia.... However bitter the British may be over the fact that they are no longer a first-class power, and are dependent on the US for their survival as an independent nation, their dog-in-the-manger attitude in South Asia is inexcusable."(FR 1951, VI, 2115-17)

Despite the rising momentum in favour of the military build-up of Pakistan, no final denouement was reached during the remaining period of the Truman administration. This was so despite the Pakistani request in July 1952 for a $2 billion credit for the purchase of US arms.(FR 1952-1954, IX, 317) Perhaps one critical factor in this outcome was the personal role of Henderson's successor, Chester Bowles, who was appointed ambassador in late 1951. A New Deal idealist, who had served as federal price administrator under Roosevelt and as governor of Connecticut, Bowles almost singlehandedly turned the deteriorating relations between the two countries on a friendly course through a popular diplomacy, manifest sincerity, and genuine warmth for India's nation-building endeavour. Of the US, Bowles asked for empathy and understanding of India's "neutralism" as a natural path, after George Washington's America, for young nations in their initial stage of national consolidation. Believing India to be really with the free world, he staunchly opposed military aid to Pakistan,(FR 1952-1954, IX, 317-19) sought to shift the regional agenda to economic development, and urged the US to assume a vital role in it. Much later, after other futile attempts in his long public career to change the course of US foreign policy in a more liberal direction, he died a disappointed man. But for now -- apart from the serious opposition the US encountered to constructing a Middle East pact from within that region itself – the thaw that Bowles brought in India-US relations and his own opposition may have dissuaded the US from proceeding with a decision on the military build-up of Pakistan, especially in the last year of a lame duck president.

The Limits to Containment

It would be a gross fallacy to infer that the pursuit of containment by a global power necessarily means extreme confrontation, perhaps to the point of physical damage to the targeted country. Even in relation to the Soviet Union, the United States desisted from preventive war or actually assisting in the liberation of the Soviet satellites in eastern Europe; indeed, detente was intermittently sought throughout the period of containment. The purpose of containment is behaviour modification so as to have the behaviour of the target state correspond to the requirements of the superpower – that is, satellisation – and not necessarily physical damage. The same end may, of course, be sought through other means as well. Consequently, it would be mistaken to expect a single universal policy of containment aimed at all middle powers. Besides, the superpower is neither completely omnipotent nor entirely unconstrained. At the same time, the target state may also have its own resources, devices and opportunities to resist and reduce the rigours of containment.

Although India's ambition for influence – beyond its capabilities and therefore unrealistic – was unacceptable and its "neutralism" anathema to the US, India posed something of a dilemma for Washington because of a variety of factors. First, there was a certain ambiguity about India's very status as a target for containment. It is one thing to adopt containment against a presumably implacable adversary, such as the USSR, with a totalitarian system and an expansionist messianic ideology, and quite another against a democratic state whose leadership proclaimed openly, and insistently, and demonstrated its dedication to modern liberal values. Indeed, all that it asked of the United States was to be true to its proclaimed democratic values, and not become the pillar of support for authoritarian regimes simply because they were ready to be dependencies of the US. Rather, it desired for the US to foster pluralism in the world and respect the autonomy of other states, and help economically the backward countries so that democracy could flourish. It felt that forced-fed military aid served only to undermine democracy through the militarisation of the politics of these countries.

Second, howsoever unacceptable its foreign policy may have been to the US, India was a nonaligned state, not – like China – a member of the Soviet bloc; indeed, it was a member of the Commonwealth, a western oriented organisation. Third, India's nonaligned status further required some moderation in containment, for to fully alienate it, or to be completely non-responsive to it, would be to drive it into the opposing bloc, an outcome that could not be deemed desirable at all. Interestingly, when India asked for the sale of 200 tanks for replacement purposes, the American embassy in New Delhi cabled its support, on the ground that it would be better for India to use American equipment than "cast about elsewhere including perhaps Soviet Union for needed military equipment."(FR 1952-1954, XI, 1661) Similarly, later, Dulles told Pakistan's Foreign Minister "it would not be good for the free world, and specifically Pakistan, if India turned to the Soviet Union for assistance."(FR 1955-1957, VIII, 405) In this manner, the larger containment of the Soviet Union served to mitigate the harshness of the containment of India. One could have perhaps posited a much harsher American treatment of India, given the same level of assertiveness on India's part, in the absence of the larger containment project aimed against the Soviet Union.

Ironically, though, at the same time, India's nonaligned status -- more accurately, its sturdy spirit of independence to resist subordination to other powers through the mechanism of military blocs -- made the US less inhibited in making decisions adverse to India, knowing that India would not go over to the other bloc. Thus National Intelligence Estimate NIE 30-54 on the probable consequences of creating a Middle East defence organisation noted: "it is extremely unlikely that India would move closer to the Soviet bloc."(FR 1952-1954, IX, 520) Many years later, during the course of the Bangladesh crisis in 1971, Kissinger, as the assistant to the president on national security, similarly felt that the US could with impunity apply unrestrained pressure on India in the sure knowledge that Mrs. Indira Gandhi would not, because of her innate nationalist commitment, subordinate the country's interests to the Soviet Union.

Fourth, India's own weakness served as a sort of strength. If lack of economic progress threatened India with political collapse and so long as the US saw the possible consequence of it a communist takeover, or if India and China were seen in a race over the merits of their respective economic-political models and so long as the US perceived the success of democracy to be in its global interests, then the US would be under some compulsion to supplement any containment of India with reinforcement of India with resources. Fifth, India's role as a nonaligned country resulted in its occupying important UN-sponsored roles in critical areas, such as Korea and Indochina; it could not thus be to the US interest to push India's alienation too far.

Indian containment, therefore, had to be a matter of some delicacy and sophistication. India seemed more like a "limited adversary", with whom both contention and cooperation had to be pursued, calling for multifold policies rather than the simple and single one of containment. Further, the global power could not take the degree of present contention or cooperation to be a permanent arrangement. For, the relationship between a global power and a middle power is a function not simply of their bilateral power position but of the total power configuration in the international system. Any change in that configuration, such as the alteration of friends and adversaries, would require the proportions of contention and cooperation to be changed. Consequently, there could be no singleminded pursuit of containment. For the same reason, the strategic cooperation on the part of the global power with the local counterweight to contain the middle power could not be completely wholehearted. As a sovereign power, the local counterweight could well change its posture depending on what served its purposes. The global power would therefore try to retain leverage over the local counterweight through various instruments, such as rationing spare parts for military equipment supplied, or keeping a modicum of relations with the middle power.

Although this study has concentrated on containment, because of the regrettable but patent neglect of it in mainstream scholarship, a fuller accounting of the American posture towards India would have to take cognisance of other aspects of the relationship, such as economic aid. However, one implication of the aspect of cooperation in the "limited adversary" relationship needs to be underlined: it inhibits announcement from the housetops of the intent at containment of the regional power.

Chapter Four
Managing the Diplomacy of Containment

It has become the accepted public view[1] – originally fostered by the US government – that military aid to Pakistan was part of the grand design for collective military defence against the Soviet military threat in the Middle East. The fact that the Truman administration had initiated plans and negotiations for, first, a Middle East Command and, then, a Middle East Defence Organisation (MEDO) lend plausibility to this view. These attempts were, of course, abandoned because of opposition from the Arab states, principally Egypt, which had been projected as the local crux of Middle East defence. Subsequently, Secretary of State Dulles came to create or accept the concept of the "northern tier", a narrower version of the earlier project in that it would exclude most of the allegedly fractious and divided Arab states, but would concentrate on those states lying close to the Soviet Union, and thus critical to military defence; particularly important were Turkey and Pakistan at the eastern and western flanks of the norther tier. Other states, it was hoped, as they come to see the dangers of Soviet aggression and the merits of collective defence would later subscribe to the resulting defence pact. One particular merit of a Turkey-Pakistan defence pact, given the apparent opposition of the two countries to communism and their determination to stand up to it, would be – even as it would draw acceptance, approval and even military aid and support from the US -- that it would seemingly be the result of local initiative; unlike the earlier

[1] John Lewis Gaddis, *Strategies of Containment: A Critical Appraisal of Postwar American National Security Policy* (New York: Oxford University Press, 1982), p. 152.

proposals, external powers would not be participants. Such has been the public view. The reality, however, seems to be more complex, if not altogether different.

The Nature of Threat in the Middle East

To begin with, the US knew that there was no military threat to the area. The Pentagon had orally told the State Department in January 1950 -- that is, before the Korean war -- that "the military strategic interests in the NEA area were now viewed as being almost negligible." It was realised that "it is doubtful that these views will be expressed in writing by JCS," but State concluded that "if the military interest in these areas is diminished to this extent, then military assistance which the United States would offer to this area should be predicated not upon the strategic aims of the United States but rather upon meeting the *political and psychological* desires of the recipient countries."(FR 1950, V, 122; emphasis added) The Korean war may have changed this situation, and indeed a Middle East defence organisation was proposed in October 1951, with US, UK, France and Turkey inviting Egypt to join in forming a Middle East Command (MEC); other states in the Middle East were expected to join later. The insensitivity to the local powers is indicated by the association of three other sponsors with the initiative -- Australia, New Zealand *and* South Africa. Egypt saw it clearly as a recipe for the continuation of foreign occupation of its territory and rejected it outright. Subsequently, the MEC concept was replaced by the more inclusive concept of MEDO. What were to be the aims of this organisation? Even as late as November 1952, the chairman of the Joint Chiefs of Staff Omar Bradley stated that "the MEDO objectives will be largely *political*." (FR 1952-1954, IX, 325; emphasis added)

"Political and psychological" aims could imply stiffening up the local backbone but still directed against Soviet designs.

However, it could also mean exercising American, if not western, influence -- indeed, in the given circumstances, control -- in the face of the rapid decline of the imperial powers of the West in that area. That this was precisely the case is made clear by the extremely broad, almost gargantuan, view of what western interests were, literally co-extensive with western control. A top secret policy statement by the National Security Council, NSC 129/1, which was approved by President Truman on April 24, 1952, makes this quite manifest. While aiming "to prevent the extension of Soviet influence and at the same time to strengthen Western influence," the statement explicitly underlined:

> Currently, the *danger* in this area to the security of the free world *arises not so much from the threat of direct Soviet military attack* as from acute instability, anti-western nationalism and Arab-Israeli antagonism which could lead to disorder and eventually to a situation in which regimes oriented toward the Soviet Union could come to power.(FR 1952-1954, IX, 222-26; emphasis added)

In other words, military aid would assure continuance in power of such elites as would allow exercise of American influence. Interestingly, one argument that American Ambassador Hildreth in Pakistan repeatedly used for providing military aid to Pakistan was that it would strengthen the government that had proven to be cooperative.(FR 1952-1954, XI, 1332, 1830) No doubt, such elites that the US supported in the Middle East would assure access to the oil resources of the area and may bring base rights as well, but the focus of concern was the threat of local nationalism, not possible Soviet aggression:

> As a means of diminishing *the threat posed by nationalistic demands* for the elimination of Western interests and by political instability in the area, the United States should make the fullest practicable use of psychological and political programmes (including special political measures) and of economic and military aid programmes and technical cooperation to influence the process of political change into channels that will effect the least compromise of Western interests and will offer the maximum promise of stable non-communist regimes.(FR 1952-1954, IX, 222-26; emphasis added)

Similarly, the National Security Council under Eisenhower also saw the threat locally in terms of its own influence rather than one emanating from the Soviet Union. Curiously, it was the local assertion of independence that the US found to be the threat. As NSC 5428 of July 23, 1954 stated:

> Current conditions and trends in the Near East are inimical to Western interests. During recent years the prestige and position of the West have declined. The nations of the Near East are *determined to assert their independence* and are suspicious of outside interest in their affairs. In particular, the influence of the United Kingdom has been weakened, with distrust and hatred replacing the former colonial subservience....
>
> In the Near East *the current danger to the security of the free world arises not so much from the threat of direct Soviet military attack as from a continuation of the present unfavourable trends*. Unless these trends are reversed, the Near East may well be lost to the West within the next few years.
>
> Efforts to prevent the loss of the Near East will require increasing responsibility, initiative, and

> leadership by the United States in the area. Even though British and French influence in the Near East has declined, the UK retains substantial interest, experience, and security positions, so that the United States will need to act in concert with the United Kingdom to the greatest extent practicable, while reserving the right to act with others (e.g., France and Turkey) or alone.(Ibid., 525-36; emphasis added)[2]

The absence of a Soviet threat was also a characteristic of assessments of South Asia; as a National Intelligence Estimate noted in June 1953: "It is not believed, however, that the Soviet Bloc would attack either Pakistan or India, except possibly in the event of general war."(FR 1952-1954, 1072-88)

That there was little local support for the endeavour for a MEDO should occasion no surprise. As one National Intelligence Estimate near the end of the Truman administration, NIE-76 of January 15, 1953, pointed out: "The US is also handicapped by the fact that the Arabs do not feel immediately threatened by the Soviet Union or recognise an immediate personal stake in the East-West struggle. They are far more apprehensive of Israeli aggression, and they suspect that Western interest in the area's defence is merely a camouflage for strengthening Western influence at the expense of their independence."(FR 1952-1954, IX, 334-43) Since the Arabs were not ready to see what was in their interest, an

[2] Interestingly, in his conversations on the Middle East with British officials in 1951, McGhee -- although a self-proclaimed "cold warrior" and an early admirer of colonialism -- was largely concerned with "the power and violence of the Nationalist movements" and how to manage them, and hardly with regional defence. Underneath these and other conversations lay a rivalry between the US and UK, even as it was often denied, over influence and control in the Middle East. George McGhee, *Envoy to the Middle World: Adventures in Diplomacy* (New York: Harper & Row, 1983), pp. 8-9, 108, 296, 338, 371. 381-87.

umbrella organisation was needed to be foisted on them in order to protect western interests, which were of a narrow kind since the western powers themselves did not see any probability of a direct physical attack by the Soviet Union. It is amazing how closely the NIE assessment of the Middle East paralleled the Indian view of US policy; as another National Intelligence Estimate underlined:

> India's leaders are jealous of India's newly won freedom of action and therefore oppose any arrangements which might entail foreign interference or foreign entanglements. They believe that India is not now a likely target of Soviet or Chinese Communist attack and that a military alliance with the West would only involve India in quarrels in which it has no direct interest.... These leaders are strong advocates of Asian nationalism and are reluctant to associate themselves with what they regard as the forces of colonialism. They believe that the Western Powers are bent on preserving their influence in Asia regardless of the interests and desires of the Asians.(FR 1951, VI, 2174-79)

For the same reasons as India's, Egypt was opposed to western-sponsored military arrangements. Nasser informed Dulles, on the latter's trip through the Middle East and South Asia in May 1953, that MEDO would be, in the eyes of the Egyptian people, a "perpetuation of occupation"; earlier, Naguib had sent Washington the message that "an arrangement replacing British forces by those of other Western countries would be merely a continuation of occupation in another form." During the trip, Dulles expressed concern that the "Arabs say there is no communist threat, merely the threat of Israel and the imperialist powers," and finally came to the conclusion -- as he cabled Eisenhower -- that MEDO "in original form is impracticable."(FR 1952-1954, IX, 21, 67, 88,

373) MEDO thus seemed undermined by nationalism.

The Special Status of Pakistan

In New Delhi, Dulles informed Nehru that MEDO was unlikely, and assured him that "the US had no present plans that would bring it into a military relationship with Pakistan which could reasonably be looked upon as unneutral as regards India." In Pakistan, Dulles emphasised to the newly appointed Prime Minister, Mohammed Ali, that he found "there was a feeling of much greater friendship in the United States for Pakistan than India," while Ali, who had until recently been ambassador in Washington, told him "of the rumour that the United States controlled him."(FR 1952-1954, IX, 121, 124) The Pakistani Army Commander in Chief Ayub Khan seemed to appeal to Dulles' hostility to communism, for Dulles -- like Acheson -- was "susceptible to Pakistan's staged anticommunism."[3] Ayub spoke to him of his fear that after Nehru India would split up and many of the parts would go over to communism, which would bring great danger for Pakistan. He further emphasised: "the United States, which admittedly is the leader of the free world today, should not be afraid to openly aid those countries which have expressed a willingness, and even desire, to cooperate with the United States.... the present Government is extremely anxious to cooperate with the United States.... if Pakistan is strengthened by United States economic and military aid, it would result in India dropping its present intransigent attitude, both toward Kashmir and other problems and even going so far as to having Nehru come to Washington in search of a settlement.... a strong Pakistan would frighten India out of her passiveness and intransigence."(FR 1952-1954, IX, 134) This was most

[3] Gaddis Smith, *Dean Acheson* (New York: Cooper Square Publishers, 1972), p. 378.

pleasing to Dulles' ears after the opposition he had encountered to MEDO in the Middle East, and seemed to underline to the US the convergence of aims in regard to India.

Dulles had not yet articulated his "northern tier" concept, but the record makes it clear that by this time Dulles had come to see the Pakistan case as one that stood apart from collective defence in the region. He cabled Washington:

> genuine feeling of friendship encountered in Pakistan which exceeded to a marked degree that encountered in any country previously visited on this trip.... Pakistan is one country that has moral courage to do its part in resisting communism.... we must find ways of maintaining steady pressure on Nehru for move by him on question of Kashmir.... Pakistan would be cooperative member of any defence scheme that may emerge in Middle East and that *we need not await formal defence arrangements as condition to some military assistance to Pakistan*. (Ibid., 147; emphasis added)

Although there is some ambiguity in the record as to the linkage of military aid for Pakistan to the development of a possible regional pact, from this point on the thrust came to centre on military aid to Pakistan, rather than regional defence. No doubt, it was important to Washington to have a regional pact as an instrument of influence and control in the region, with as many client states as possible, but strictly in terms of concrete military aid what was important was Pakistan alone, and possibly Iraq, which in the local rivalries of the Middle East was the potential counterweight to Egypt, much as Pakistan was to India in South Asia. There was, undoubtedly, the underlying thought that initiation of military aid to Pakistan may well generate a band-wagon effect, with other states stampeding to join up with the US. Once adherence to some notion of regional pact would make apparent the connection of its bringing in economic and military aid, then other states would presumably quickly line up to join. As one National Intelligence Estimate saw it:

> a regional grouping based on the Turk-Pakistani agreement would be less subject to the stigma of being under direct Western control than were the Middle East Command and Middle East Defence Organisation. The desire for US military and economic aid is probably the most powerful inducement to enter into such an arrangement, and the willingness of individual states to join will depend largely on the nature, scale, and terms of the US aid offered them.(FR 1952-1954, IX, 516-20)

But, who would be chosen by the US to receive aid would be determined by it in the light of its own interests in the region and the world, not in that of some abstract comprehensive principle of regional defence. In any case, while a regional pact would be desirable, it was not essential – military aid to Pakistan was imperative in its own terms, regardless of the potentiality of a regional pact and the possible impact of a military arrangement with Pakistan on the development of a regional pact. No doubt, the US as a global power saw its military aid to Pakistan from the perspective of its own worldwide goals, but gradually the course of diplomacy was turned on its head: it was not so much that military aid was to be provided to Pakistan as part of a regional pact as it was that a regional pact needed to be created in order to provide a diplomatic cover for the military aid to Pakistan.

The decision to extend military aid to Pakistan thus became a prior one, and it was taken in Washington, but then the US organised an extraordinary orchestration of diplomacy to force a regional arrangement into place as an umbrella for the military aid in a valiant bid to confuse and defuse opposition. Equally, the United States launched an amazing disinformation campaign to demonstrate that all this had been thought up by the local powers in the region for collective defence, and that Washington could not but be responsive to this display of regional initiative to counter the Soviet threat.

With the abandonment of MEDO, the US came to accept the rationale for a "northern tier" pact, stretching from Turkey to Pakistan. But, despite claims to its utility in covering the southern rim around the Soviet Union, by the time of the decision on military aid to Pakistan, the concept had in American thinking boiled down to just Pakistan – surprisingly, a state which had no border with the Soviet Union since Iran and Afghanistan stood as buffers between it and the USSR. As Turkey was already a member of NATO, its aherence to a "northern tier" pact was not going to add anything new. Meanwhile, the US ruled Iran and Afghanistan out of consideration, for fear of provoking the Soviet Union and also because of the supposed political and military weakness of the countries in effectively fulfilling an allegedly defence role. In fact, in Iran the political situation was not entirely certain after the US-directed ouster of Mossadegh. On the other hand, the US could not really accommodate Afghanistan, given Pakistan's antagonism towards it over the Pushtunistan dispute. Iraq, near the other end of the tier, would be useful, but the US was not too enthusiastic. Indeed, when Iraq subsequently showed some unusual enterprise in organising collective defence of its own interpretation, there was anger in Washington, with a warning that Iraq desist from that course on pain of losing US military aid. Note, for example, Dulles' memorandum of August 23, 1954 to Assistant Secretary Byroade:

> I am greatly disturbed over the report that Iraq is planning a security pact with Egypt and is moving away from the idea of joining up with Turkey and Pakistan.

> We bought the idea of military aid to Iraq on the theory that it was going to tie up with the northern tier countries and not merely build up the Arab League as againt Israel.
>
> When the Iraqi Prime Minister was here, he told me of the projected union with Syria and Lebanon, and I told him that because this would bring their influence to the Israel border, I thought it should be preceded by their moving along with Turkey and Pakistan. I understood him to indicate that he would do so. Now this proposal of joining with Egypt to strengthen the Arab Collective Security Pact comes up. I frankly do not like it and I believe it might cause us to invoke the Iraq Mutual Security Agreement provision that we may review our military aid in the light of the international situation at the time.(Ibid., 545)

It is noteworthy, on the other hand, that Great Britain was encouraged by the prospect of Iraqi-Egyptian cooperation in that "non-Westerners were suggesting a regional organisation that would invite Western participation."(Ibid., 546) What American opposition demonstrated was that military aid and membership in American-sponsored regional organisations were contingent on serving American interests, as defined by the US, not regional purposes.

In the final analysis, for now, the US was left to take recourse to linking Turkey, which was already committed through NATO, with Pakistan -- two states at the extreme ends of the northern tier, with no territory contiguous to each other. In the meantime, the focus came to rest entirely on military aid to Pakistan. Discussions in the National Security Council in June and July confirmed the inclination to go ahead with extending military aid to it. In late September, General Ayub Khan came to the US on an extended visit and discussed the issue with State and Defence officials. Matters began to move with greater speed, and a decision was now imminent. Then on Christmas eve in 1953 began a spectacular orchestration of secret diplomacy by the US to mask the decision as a response to local initiative for collective defence. In a top secret telegram to the American Ambassador in Turkey – Avra Warren, who had until November 1952 been ambassador in Pakistan – Dulles stated:

> Decision on extension of military assistance to Pakistan has not as yet been made by the US Government. Before requesting such a decision *we wish to determine procedures to be followed in the event it is decided to go ahead. Conceivably the type of procedure that could be worked out might have a bearing upon the decision itself.*
>
> We think *best way would be in form of support for some sort of regional defence cooperation initiated by states in the area.* Believe this important both domestically and abroad *to provide rationale for extension military aid programmes* beyond present geographical limits and to support our contention that assistance to Pakistan is directed toward defence against outside aggression and not against India or Afghanistan.
>
> ....you approach Turks in greatest confidence without delay along following lines:
>
> ....It seems to us that *one way to minimise political repercussions* and maximise Pakistani area defence contribution *might be to link US aid programme with initiation of mutual defence arrangements between Turkey and Pakistan* and any other states in the area which might be interested and acceptable to first two. *This would show that intent of US aid is to strengthen area defence against outside aggression* rather than to take sides in

disputes within area such as those that exist between Pakistan and her neighbours. Early creation of regional arrangement would have further advantage of enabling a start on regional defence planning which is highly desirable from military viewpoint.

....We do not believe time has yet come for inclusion of Iran or Afghanistan in such an arrangement. Similarly, most Arab states are too preoccupied with Palestine and other disputes with West to be ready join anything savouring of Middle East Defence Organisation, even without direct Western participation. We have however some reason to believe Iraq would not be unreceptive to defence planning, despite negative attitude of other Arabs.... We would not however consider her participation need be a condition precedent to establishment of arrangement between Turkey and Pakistan.

....If that decision is to go ahead and if Turks concur in general desirability of Turk-Pakistani defence arrangement as suggested above, we shall want to concert with Turks on tactics. We think it would be undesirable for US to take any public initiative. Either Turkey or Pakistan could lead off by proposing (to the other) exploratory bilateral talks. These might be secret at first but at some fairly early stage it would seem desirable that the two parties publicly announce their intention to negotiate. Simultaneously or shortly afterward Pakistan could make formal request for US military aid and we could make public favourable response based on idea of supporting collective security as exemplified by proposed Turk-Pakistani pact.(FR 1952-1954, IX, 439-41; emhasis added)

Similarly, on December 29, after hearing from Turkey, Dulles asked the American ambassador in Pakistan to inform the prime minister in complete secrecy:

> 1. Turkish Government being informed we considering military aid programme for Pakistan.
>
> 2. We believe it desirable minimise political repercussions (India and Afghanistan) and maximise Pakistan contribution area defence. One way do this would be to link US aid to initiation of mutual defence understanding between Turkey and Pakistan. Such an arrangement might be open-ended permitting addition of others if agreed to....
>
> 4. If PM asks *whether this means we will not extend aid unless Turkey goes along you may say this is not necessarily so* but that you are sure the US will wish to look at the problem in light of Turkish reaction.(Ibid., 441-42; emphasis added)

On an earlier occasion, near the end of the Truman administration, Turkey had been opposed to Pakistan's membership in MEDO "because of possible strong adverse reactions from India and Afghanistan."(Ibid., 317) Now, however, after further discussions in the intervening period with the US and Pakistan, its response was different. That response -- as summarised by the State Department's historians -- succinctly underlined Washington's intent: "the U.S. Government, while hoping an agreement between Turkey and Pakistan would contribute to the formation of an organisation for the defence of the Middle East, considered *the immediate aim of an agreement to be the possibility of providing military aid to Pakistan without arousing adverse reactions in the international field*." (Ibid., 448; emphasis added) This time Turkey was ready to oblige. However, it was unwilling to enter into a binding military alliance with Pakistan on the objection that "Pakistan did not constitute a geographic entity or strategic unit with Turkey."(Ibid., 455) All that it would countenance was an agreement for consultation, not a defence agreement. But, in its desperate need for a cover for the military aid to Pakistan, Washington was ready to accept this feeble arrangement for the facade of regional defence and local initiative it provided; it reminded Turkey:

> Re form of arrangement between Turkey and Pakistan it is, of course, for Turks to decide form agreement may appropriately take. Department wishes recall, however, that when Turks originally consulted point was made that *best way for US give military aid Pakistan would be in form of support for some form of regional defence cooperation initiated by states in area*. It was Department's understanding that Turks agreed to and endorsed this proposal.(Ibid., 464; emphasis added)

Washington realised that the proposed agreement did not constitute a satisfactory arrangement, but was willing to stretch its meaning for its purpose and was ready to live with it:

> With Pakistan request for military aid following closely on Turk-Pak communique re talks and US reply pegged to this, Department considers that defence implications of arrangements will be clear. Although Department has no objection to avoidance term "defence" and placing main emphasis agreement in political field, hopes that Turks will at least feel able use phrase "security cooperation agreement".... This would be helpful in presentation of case for US arms assistance. We prepared, of course, accept Turkey's position this matter....(Ibid.)

Turkey wished also to extend the deal to Afghanistan and wanted Washington to provide military aid to that country, but Washington demurred, underlining once again the priority for aid to Pakistan over any notion of regional defence:

> If Turkey proposes agreement with Afghanistan similar to one with Pakistan, this might prove embarrassing to US at this time since *we expect to use Pak-Turk agreement as framework for Pakistan military aid*. (Ibid., 466)

As it got wind of the proposal for military aid to Pakistan, India stridently voiced its opposition, but Dulles told Eisenhower to stand firm:

> The Secretary gave the President again a general summary of his thinking in which he stressed the effect, now that Nehru had raised strong public objection, of not going ahead. He stated that in his opinion *this one act would do a great deal to establish Nehru as the leader of all South and Southeast Asia and nations in that area would henceforth be reluctant to proceed on matters with the West without obtaining Nehru's support*. The Secretary mentioned certain instances of the past where Asiatic nations had supported our position in defiance of India, particularly in the UN and Japanese Peace Treaty. He felt that the attitude of these nations would certainly be affected if we should bow to India in this public issue.(Ibid., 453-54; emphasis added)

Having obtained the concurrence of Turkey, Washington then planned the whole diplomatic operation and news management to the last detail, while all the time proclaiming the opposite of what was happening -- local initiative:

I. Joint Turk-Pakistani announcement to be made after following steps.

1. Turks will approach Pakistanis Karachi with proposal two Governments undertake promptly negotiation agreement providing for consultation political, economic and security matters of mutual interest. US Ambassador will offer secret assurances that US ready provide aid within framework such agreement. We expect Turk approach will be made during present week, and hope for joint announcement next week.

2. Prior public announcement, Turks would sound Iraqis as to their interest joining proposed arrangements. We would inform Iraq of our support arrangement, our hope Iraq will feel able cooperate, and our intention supply Iraq military assistance.

3. Two-three days prior joint announcement, Turks (and presumably Pakistanis) would inform Iraq, India, Afghanistan. Turks would make special effort, which we would support, to reassure Afghanistan.

4. Turks would make explanatory statement NAC not later than day joint communique. We would support Turk position, and hope British and French would do same. (British already fully informed and French will be briefed by Turks and Department within next day or so.)

II. Announcement US intention supply military assistance Pakistan would be prepared by following moves:

1. US would comment favourably on Turkish-Pakistani communique but in manner consistent our purpose emphasising indigenous character development. Hope British, French offer similar comment. Several days later Pakistan would publicly

> request US military aid.
>
> 2. Prior our reply Pakistan (perhaps by one day), India would be informed of decision, and personal letter from President would be handed Nehru.
>
> 3. Public announcement US reply to Pakistan request would be in form Presidential statement. Would be issued within two or three days receipt Pakistani request.(Ibid., 473-74)

Washington further warned its officials "of the danger of making public comments in such a way as to suggest the United States Government has played a prominent role in promoting it."(Ibid., 480) In cable after cable to its embassies, Washington underlined that it was "important that indigenous character of venture should be emphasised. Although US interest has been shown from start and we have given encouragement, Department convinced US should remain as far in background as possible. US representatives should follow this line in their official contacts."(Ibid., 484) Finally, in the latter part of February 1954, came the public announcement of the American decision to provide military aid to Pakistan. The US at the same time offered military aid to India as well, but it was simply another tactic to soften Indian opposition since nowhere in the record was there ever a serious discussion of that proposition.

The Consequences of Divergent Goals

If one purpose in giving military aid is to obtain influence through the internal leverage it provides, then the United States succeeded admirably. Soon after the US and Pakistan signed the agreement on military aid, American Ambassador Horace Hildreth in Pakistan informed Washington:

> This closer relationship between Pakistan and the United States, while openly aligning this government with the forces of the free world, has at the same time increased the expectations of the Government of Pakistan and produced a feeling akin to one of dependence on the United States.(FR 1952-1954, XI, 1851)

As a consequence, Pakistan was subsequently led into entering the Baghdad Pact and SEATO, becoming in the process "America's most allied ally." Still later, the dependence became even deeper, for -- as the American embassy in Karachi informed Washington -- "only reason why Pakistan able keep going is US aid."(FR 1955-1957, VIII, 484) One consequence of the dependence was American intrusion in local politics. Hildreth -- whose daughter was married to the son of Pakistani President Iskander Mirza -- became a powerful figure in the country's political system, so much so that a popular slogan in Pakistan claimed "real Pak Prime Minister is named Hildreth." For his part, while informing Washington of having told President Mirza "and it will be made clear to Suhrawardy by others, that US has no objection inclusion Suhrawardy in high Cabinet post," he added: "fact is that US relationship so important to Pakistanis that complete non-involvement impossible."(FR 1955-1957, VIII, 434)

It was, however, left to his successor, James Langley, to tear off the veil on the military aid; in a brilliant wide-ranging analysis of the Pakistani situation, he pointed out: "I fear that it would not be too difficult to make a rather convincing case that the present military programme is based on *a hoax, the hoax being that it is related to the Soviet threat.*" (FR 1955-1957, VIII, 487-90; emphasis added) Langley, however, thought he was making a new discovery -- whereas the record shows US officialdom to have known all along -- when he said:

> One of the most disturbing attitudes I have encountered in the highest political places here is that the United States *must* keep up and increase its aid to Pakistan, and conversely, that Pakistan is doing the US a favour in accepting aid, in addition to the Pakistan pro-western posture in the Baghdad Pact and SEATO and the UN, when actually these postures are in part dictated by Pakistan hatred for India.

In calling it "in part," the ambassador was still being generous. For, it had been obvious to US officials since long ago as to why Pakistan was so eager to cooperate with the US, but they chose to suppress their suspicions in view of the *political* goals of the US in extending military aid. The Joint Chiefs of Staff had discounted early on any Soviet threat and continued to maintain into 1956 that they "foresee no Soviet aggression in this area as a separate action. It would only occur if there were a global war." At the same time, while believing that "the Russian capacity is exaggerated," they thought that the maintenance of ground troops by the countries immediately involved, sufficiently strong to stop the Russians, would break the economies of the countries in question."(FR 1955-1957, VIII, 464) On the other hand, besides expanding force levels and re-equipping existing formations, Pakistan kept escalating its demands for advanced weaponry, asking for light bombers and submarines. The Pakistan prime minister told Secretary Dulles and his colleagues, "his motives were similar to those of the US in wanting a nuclear bomb deterrent to Soviet aggression... he wanted light bombers as a deterrent against possible Indian aggression.... the Pakistan Air Force had now absorbed fighters and that bombers were the logical next step."(Ibid. 483) West Pakistan Governor Gurmani told roving US ambassador James Richards, "When Pakistanis speak of 'defence' they speak of defence against India."(Ibid., 477)

But US officials had not only known prior to the military aid as to what Pakistan's purposes were, but also were aware of what the impact of their military aid to Pakistan would be; one National Intelligence Estimate had noted in June 1953 that, while India had no incentive to go to war with Pakistan, "if Pakistan's military capabilities should be significantly increased as a result of such a military agreement, Pakistan's leaders might consider an attack on India."(FR 1952-1954, XI, 1072-88)

Since the US and Pakistan had entered into the deal with different purposes rather than as a result of a community of interests as in NATO, there was necessarily confusion about its relationship to military preparedness. As Assistant Secretary of Defence Struve Hensel noted a whole year after the decision:

> It was perfectly obvious that no member of the Country Team had any clear idea of the part Pakistan was expected to play in the defence of the Middle East or whether that role would be developed into an important one. There was continual reference to the fact that Admiral Radford favoured increased military strength in Pakistan, but no one seemed to know precisely why except that Pakistani obviously make reliable fighting soldiers. At the same time, it seems quite clear that Pakistan regards the Indian threat as much more serious, than the Russian or Communist China threats. The Pakistani Army is now deployed along the Indian border and all tactical and strategic planning by the Pakistani centre on Indian problems as having first priority.(FR 1955-1957, VIII, 419)

The US was thus fully a partner in Pakistan's military aims against India even as it now began worrying about having triggered an arms race on the subcontinent, with deleterious consequences for economic development. However, the impact of military aid on Pakistan's political system was no less serious, apart from the American intrusion into its politics. As Pakistan increasingly resorted to authoritarian measures, the embassy in Karachi informed Washington that the trends "would lead many to conclude that representative regime cannot exist in same system with expanded Pakistan military strength."(FR 1955-1957, VIII, 479) However, it was left to the ever hard-nosed Langley to articulate the problem with savage clarity:

> over-all situation in Pakistan is deteriorating while military programmes may be proceeding satisfactorily. Military strength, without a sound economic and political base, does not constitute real strength in South Asia or elsewhere. It is time to rethink our approach.... A more comprehensive review, however, is called for, which should give greater weight to developing Pakistan as a strong viable ally of the US rather than concentrating on building of a military force which may not have vis-a-vis Communist bloc a value in proportion with its cost both to Pakistan and to US.(FR 1955-57, VIII, 486)

That had been precisely Nehru's point to the US all along – and also of some remarkable Americans such as Chester Bowles.

Summary and Conclusions

It would be fatuous to underestimate the US concern with the containment of the Soviet Union and, in the cause of "collective" defence, extending military aid to countries on the Soviet periphery. But the apotheosisation of Soviet containment as an explanation for American activities in different regions of the world neglects the autonomous importance of regional factors in American calculations about its own drive for influence and control. Of course, any decision that moves through a complex bureaucratic process is likely to involve multifold ends. But sufficient and compelling evidence has been advanced in this study on the US decision to provide military aid to Pakistan to demonstrate that considerations of American rivalry for influence with the regional power, India – quite independently of any containment of the Soviet Union – were heavily implicated in the decision. Pakistan, bolstered by military aid, was intended to serve as a local counterweight on behalf of the US against India even though the aim was sought to be mystified through its association with collective defence in the Middle East. The evidence is too massive to be simply dismissed. As against the weighty evidence presented in this study, it is not unreasonable to ask: What evidence does the orthodox position have in its defence other than the *official public* statements of the government? And how do its proponents account for the accumulated weight of the classified evidence now available that runs counter to their proposition?

From the perspective of the US attempt to build local counterweights against regional rivals, the containment of the Soviet Union -- rather than being a special category, which then became the governing framework, determining US policies in different regions – appears as only a sub-category of the general category of containment on the part of a hegemonic global power, aimed at all actual or aspirant independent centres of power. In that light, the Soviet Union emerges as one among several targets of containment, though the most spectacular one.[1] The documentary record thus confirms the revisionist interpretation on the containment of regional rivals on the part of the US. Understandably, containment is not the only policy that the global power pursues towards its regional rivals for influence, nor need it be taken to be permanent, though it may well be, depending on the changing configuration of power.

There could perhaps be a counter-argument, as against the position advanced in this study, that the American containment of India was not an action addressed to India primarily, but followed as a necessary subsidiary consequence of the larger containment of the Soviet Union. In other words, the United States -- convinced of the immense threat that it perceived as emanating from the Soviet Union -- had perforce to militarily organise every region of the world.

[1] On the basis of archival research, one scholar makes the point that "the Baghdad Pact was more a product of Anglo-American rivalries for supremacy than a well-considered military strategy to bolster Middle Eastern and South Asian defences against a Soviet attack.... the Baghdad Pact does not appear to have improved either the stability or the security of the Middle East and South Asia. It did, however, create the conditions for US domination over the two regions. This raises a central question: did the Baghdad Pact, despite its many failings, mark the United States' final victory over Great Britain during the Cold War, a victory which the Suez Crisis of 1956 merely served to confirm?" See Ayesha Jalal, "Towards the Baghdad Pact: South Asia and the Middle East Defence in the Cold War, 1947-1955," *International History Review*, IX, no. 3 (August 1989), 409-33. The notion that the containment of Great Britain, indeed, preceded that of the Soviet Union was first made by the revisionist historian Gabriel Kolko, *The Roots of American Foreign Policy: An Analysis of Power and Purpose* (Boston: Beacon Press, 1969).

Accordingly, any power that refused to join in this enormous enterprise of containment of the Soviet Union weakened the collective effort at defence of the western world. Indeed, if regional powers additionally attempted to rally others to stay away from the momentous challenge facing the western world, they could seriously damage the collective enterprise. Such a development was, however, fundamentally intolerable for the global power, given its responsibilities for world peace and welfare. Every power had therefore to be brought under the umbrella of military arrangements organised and presided over by the US as security manager. No power could be left outside these arrangements, leave aside being allowed to build its own sphere of influence. In these circumstances, regional powers were required to be contained for the sake of the higher interests of the western world, including perhaps the real interests of the regional powers, of which they may not be fully cognisant themselves. Such a containment, however, was not primarily directed as such at regional powers, but essentially followed from the broader containment of the Soviet Union; it was not an end in itself but only a means. It may well be that, once initiated in this manner, regional containment may have acquired a dynamic of its own, especially under pressure from the sponsored local counterweight, but that policy was to begin with simply the consequence of containment of the Soviet Union.[2]

It would be difficult to discount the notion that some such calculations as the counter-argument envisages may have underlain American policy toward regional powers. It seems, however, that the vision of the organisation of the world that underlies the counter-argument really certifies an attempt at global satellisation and bespeaks of a global power that is not simply reactive but is in reality enormously activist. The resulting posture of the global power can be considered

[2] This line of thought is a result of self-reflection on the argument, reinforced by a suggestion by my colleague, Professor Paul Noble.

reactive only in the sense of a resolve to quash any resistance to the imposition of its will. Such a breathtakingly grandiose vision connotes an extraordinarily activist foreign policy, which is intolerant of pluralism or diversity in the world. Inspired really more by ambition than by fear, it could brook no variation in foreign policy behaviour on the part of other powers, who were otherwise so weak and fragile in their capabilities. What such a vision demanded was that every power subordinate its own interpretation of international reality and of its national interests to the single one held by the US. In other words, every power had to either become satellised willingly or suffer containment at the hands of the United States.

Such an all-encompassing view of America's posture toward the rest of the non-communist world cannot but raise doubts once again about the veracity of the professedly reactive foundations of containment policy aimed against the Soviet Union. Could it not be that the containment of the Soviet Union, rather than being reactive, partook of the same activist posture that became manifest in relation to the non-communist world? Indeed, containment of a power that had been devastated economically and demographically by war could not be anything but part of an activist policy.

At any rate, whether the containment of a regional power that refused to follow the US interpretation of international reality was only a subsidiary function of containment of the Soviet Union, or it was a principal function of the general posture of containment toward all independent centres of power, is perhaps unresolvable at such a high level of generality. More to the point is the abundance of evidence testifying to the fact that specifically a regional power – which refused to follow American leadership in its own region, ten thousand miles away from the shores of the US – was perceived as rebellious in its refusal to become satellised, and was therefore deemed a suitable target for containment. To be sure, it may be countered that containment was the necessary comeuppance for the insolence of the regional power in challenging the hegemonic global power. That, however, simply underlines the drastic difference between the positions and perspectives of global and regional powers, precisely the premise that has served as the basis for the analytical framework for this study. Furthermore, from the perspective of the middle power, it matters little whether its containment was subsidiary to Soviet containment, or was independent of it. What matters, in the ultimate analysis, is that containment was in fact pursued – regardless of its origins – in relation to regional powers which were neither ideologically communist nor aligned with the Soviet Union. The record is explicit on the point that containment specifically of regional powers was pursued because they were seen as rivals to American influence and control.

Regrettably, however, the US pursuit of containment of regional powers has been met with studied neglect in mainstream American scholarship, which has been seemingly more comfortable with containment of an evil communist empire by a presumably benign hegemonic global power. The accepted framework of realism has been admirably suited for the purpose, showing a heroic status quo power resisting a determined imperialist power. It may well be that the superpower conflict has attracted greater attention because the fate of the world has been tied up with it. However, this preoccupation has never prevented the study by American scholars of the numerous regional conflicts in the Third World. It seems that American scholarship is really less comfortable with the US containment of regional powers, which is likely to reveal not so benign motives. It has neglected to use in a critical mannner the same framework of realism to understand the impulses behind the state behaviour of the US as an activist power, rather than simply a reactive one, though the prewar American record in Latin America ought to have compellingly led it in that direction. The official understanding of US international behaviour has, as a result, acquired the proportions of "hegemony" (in the Gramscian sense) in academia.

It is to be wondered if this state of affairs is a consequence of American scholars being involved in various capacities in the work of the United States government. Certainly, where eminent scholars serve the government in high office, such as Secretary of State or assistant to the president, it creates a powerful intellectual updraft throughout academia for scholarship to correspond to official ideology. In the circumstance, research problems that are likely to lead to the questioning of the official interpretation may well then be avoided. In that case, scholarship simply becomes a handmaiden of government rather than an intellectual pursuit in the cause of knowledge. The almost automatic dismissal -- through nothing more than assertions[3] -- by American scholars of the revisionist interpretation of US motivations in the decision to extend military aid to Pakistan may well have other sources, but it is impressive that much of the writing on the

[3] The tradition continues. A recent work states: "Washington was not interested in backing Pakistan against either India or Afghanistan, although the United States considered that Pakistan's role in containment, particularly in support of Iran and Turkey, a much higher priority than the maintenance of good relations with New Delhi or Kabul. To attain the former, Washington had to make concessions on the latter, which *New Delhi interpreted as motivated by anti-Indian objectives*. Although *India was wrong on the motivation*, it was right about the consequences: the US-Pakistani alliance played only an incidental role in containing communism -- and then only into the early 1960s -- while allowing Pakistan to take much stronger positions in its disputes with India and Afghanistan than would otherwise have been possible." See Richard Sisson and Leo E. Rose, *War and Secession: Pakistan, India, and the Creation of Bangladesh* (Berkeley: University of California Press, 1990), pp. 47-48; emphasis added. Apart from the fact that the stance on motivation was the US government's public line, one wonders what is the logic and evidence for this conclusion.

Similarly, others simply attribute to India the suspicion that the US aim was to limit, contain or neutralise Indian influence, but

American relationship with South Asia in the US has come from academics who have served the United States government in various capacities.

implicitly assume American innocence in this regard even as they avoid seriously dealing with the merits of the case. See, for example: "American policy toward Pakistan was never driven by concern about India. However, New Delhi has consistently seen the US-Pakistani relationship less as an alliance against the Soviet Union than one directed against itself, or, in recent decades, as a de facto Sino-Pakistani-US entente against India." Paul Kreisberg, "The United States, South Asia and American Interests," *Journal of International Affairs*, vol. 43, no. 1 (Summer/Fall 1989), pp. 83-95. And also: "...criticism of the United States, at relatively little cost, wins favour among the elements of the Indian left. This has led Indian leaders to conjure up images of America as bent on 'containing' India's growing power through support of its enemies...." Robert L. Hardgrave, Jr., "Linkage Politics in India: The Relationship of Domestic Politics to Foreign Policy," in Robert A. Scalapino, et al., *Asia and the Major Powers: Domestic Politics and Foreign Policy* (Berkeley: Institute of East Asian Studies, University of California, 1988), pp. 306-40. For an earlier example, see the letter by William J. Barnds and W. Howard Wriggins in *Foreign Policy*, No. 20 (Fall 1975), pp. 250-53.

Appendix
A Note on the New Evidence

Chapter 3 on *The Intellectual Heritage from the Truman Administration* and chapter 4 on *Managing the Diplomacy of Containment* are based entirely on new evidence that was either not available or not accessible at the time that the initial argument was made in *American Geopolitics and India* (New Delhi: Manohar, 1976) and in the two chapters in John W. Mellor (ed.), *India: A Rising Middle Power* (Boulder, Colorado: Westview Press, 1979), chapters 5-6. The new evidence consists chiefly of selected classified documents of the US Government, published by the Department of State in its series on *Foreign Relations of the United States.* The volumes relied on here are primarily for the years 1949 (vol. VI), 1950 (vol. V), 1951 (vol. VI), 1952-1954 (vols. IX and XI), and 1955-1957 (vol. VIII), published respectively in 1977, 1978, 1977, 1986 and 1983, and 1987.

There is in a couple of instances reliance in Chapter 3 also on documents excerpted in Rajendra K. Jain (ed.), *US-South Asian Relations, 1947-82* (New Delhi: Radiant Publishers, 1983), which in these particular cases were in turn drawn from the heavily-documented study by M.S. Venkataramani, *The American Role in Pakistan* (New Delhi: Radiant Publishers, 1983).

Chapter 2 on *Motives in the Eisenhower Administration*, while including some earlier evidence based on secondary sources, has two additional important primary sources. One of these is new, consisting of the memoirs of the Canadian diplomat, Escott Reid, *Envoy to Nehru* (Delhi: Oxford University Press, 1981). Besides their own inherent value, these memoirs were instrumental in directing attention to the other primary source that had not been utilised earlier: the two valuable despatches by Robert Trumbull, which appeared in the *New York Times*, December 9 and 10, 1953, and reveal Vice President Nixon's thinking on Nehru and Indian foreign policy.

Parts of Chapter 1 on *The Contending Perspectives on Motivation* -- "Analytical Framework on Great Power-Middle Power Interaction" and "US Policy on Containment: Global and Regional" – draw on earlier work for the sake of offering a unified argument.

Select Bibliography

Acheson, Dean. *Present at the Creation*. New York: W.W. Norton and Co., 1969.

Barnds, William J. "Comment," in John W. Mellor (ed.). *India: A Rising Middle Power*. Boulder, Colorado: Westview Press, 1979.

______. *India, Pakistan and the Major Powers*. New York: Praeger Publishers, 1972.

Barnds, William J. and W. Howard Wriggins. Letter. *Foreign Policy*, No. 20 (Fall 1975), pp. 250-53.

Bell, Coral. *Survey of International Affairs 1954*. London: Oxford University Press, 1957.

Bowles, Chester. *Promises to Keep: My Years in Public Life 1941-1969*. New York: Harper & Row, 1971.

Cohen, Stephen P. and Richard L. Park. *India: Emergent Power?* New York: Crane, Russak & Co., 1978.

Das, Durga. *From Curzon to Nehru & After*. London: Wm. Collins, Sons and Co., 1969.

Diebel, Terry L. and John Lewis Gaddis (ed.). *Containing the Soviet Union: A Critique of US Policy*. Washington, DC: Pergamon-Brassey's International Defence Publishers, 1987.

Gaddis, John Lewis. *Strategies of Containment: A Critical Appraisal of Postwar American National Security Policy*. New York: Oxford University Press, 1982.

Gulin, Michael A. *John Foster Dulles: A Statesman and His Times*. New York: Columbia University Press, 1972.

Harrison, Selig S. "America, India, and Pakistan: A Chance for a Fresh Start," *Harper's*, No. 233 (July 1966).

______. "India, Pakistan and the U.S.--II," *New Republic*, No. 141 (August 24, 1959).

Jain, Rajendra K. (ed.). *US-South Asian Relations, 1947-1982.* New Delhi: Radiant Publishers, 1983.

Kalb, Marvin and Bernard Kalb. *Kissinger*. Boston: Little, Brown and Co., 1974.

Larson, Deborah Welch. *Origins of Containment: A Psychological Explanation*. Princeton: Princeton University Press, 1985.

Liska, George. *States in Evolution: Changing Societies and Traditional Systems in World Politics*. Baltimore: Johns Hopkins University Press, 1973.

______. "The Third World: Regional Systems and Global Order," in Robert E. Osgood et al. *Retreat From Empire*. Baltimore: Johns Hopkins University Press, 1973.

Lord, Winston. "America's Purposes in an Ambiguous Age," in Department of State, *Bulletin*, No. 1845 (November 4, 1974).

McGhee, George. *Envoy to the Middle World: Adventures in Diplomacy*. New York: Harper & Row, 1983.

McMahon, Robert J. "United States Cold War Strategy in South Asia: Making a Military Commitment to Pakistan, 1947-1954," *The Journal of American History*, vol. 75, no. 3 (December 1988), pp. 812-840.

Middleton, Drew. *Retreat From Victory*. New York: Hawthorn Books, 1973.

Nayar, Baldev Raj. "A World Role: The Dialectics of Purpose and Power," in John W. Mellor (ed.). *India: A Rising Middle Power*. Boulder, Colorado: Westview Press, 1979. Chapter 5.

______. *American Geopolitics and India*. New Delhi: Manohar, 1976.

______. "Treat India Seriously," *Foreign Policy*, No. 18 (Sprint 1975), pp. 133-54.

Nayar, Kuldip. *India After Nehru*. Delhi: Vikas Publications, 1975.

New York Times. December 9 and 10, 1953, and September 13, 1976.

Palmer, Norman D. Review. *American Political Science Review.*, vol. 72 (1978), p. 1177.

Reid, Escott. *Envoy to Nehru*. Delhi: Oxford University Press, 1981.

Schoultz, Lars. *National Security and United States Policy Toward Latin America*. Princeton: Princeton University Press, 1987.

Sisson, Richard. "Pakistan and U.S. Foreign Policy Formulation: Interest, Perception, and the Context of Choice," in Leo E. Rose and Noor A. Husain (ed.). *United States-Pakistan Relations*. Berkeley, CA: Institute of East Asian Studies, University of California, 1985.

Sisson, Richard and Leo E. Rose. *War and Secession: Pakistan, India, and the Creation of Bangladesh*. Berkeley: University of California Press, 1990.

Smith, Gaddis. *Dean Acheson*. New York: Cooper Square Publishers, 1972.

Toledano, Ralph de. *Nixon*. New York: Henry Holt, 1956.

Tucker, Robert W. *The Radical Left and American Foreign Policy*. Baltimore: Johns Hopkins University Press, 1971.

Trumbull, Robert. "U.S. Faces Decision on Major Asia Ties," *New York Times*, December 9, 1953, p. 3.

———. "Pakistan Eyed as Balance," *New York Times*, December 10, 1953, p. 2.

U.S. Congress, House, Committee on International Relations. *The Persian Gulf, 1975*. Hearings, 94th Congress, 1st Session, 1975.

U.S. Congress, Senate, Committee on Foreign Relations. *Foreign Assistance Authorisation*. Hearings, 93rd Congress, 2nd Session, 1974.

U.S. Department of State. *Bulletin*, XXX, No. 768 (March 15, 1954), pp. 400-401.

U.S. Department of State. *Foreign Relations of the United States, 1949: Volume VI: The Near East, South Asia, and Africa*. Washington, DC: 1977.

______. *Foreign Relations of the United States, 1950: Volume V: The Near East, South Asia, and Africa.* Washington, DC: 1978.

______. *Foreign Relations of the United States, 1951: Volume VI: Asia and the Pacific.* Washington, DC: 1977

______. *Foreign Relations of the United States, 1952-1954: Volume IX: The Near East and Middle East.* Washington, DC: 1986.

______. *Foreign Relations of the United States, 1952-1954: Volume XI: Africa and South Asia.* Washington, DC: 1983.

______. *Foreign Relations of the United States, 1955-1957: Volume VIII: South Asia.* Washington, DC: 1987.

Venkataramani, M.S. *The American Role in Pakistan.* New Delhi: Radiant Publishers, 1983.

Waggoner, Walter H. "Nixon Due to Urge Pakistan Arms Aid," *New York Times*, December 10, 1953, p. 1.

Index